DATE DUE

FEB 1 3 1974

SHAKESPEARE AND "DEMI-SCIENCE"

AMS PRESS
NEW YORK

THE FRONTISPIECE of this volume is a reproduction of the Felton Portrait of Shakespeare, which was bought for five guineas from a dealer in antiquities in 1792, and came into the possession of the well-known Shakespeare scholar, George Steevens. The original was painted on a wood panel some eleven inches by eight and bore on the back the inscription "Gul. Shakespear[e], 1597. R. B.," these initials intended to suggest Richard Burbage, the famous actor who is believed to have painted the portrait of Shakespeare, an engraving of which by Droeshout appears on the title page of the first folio of Shakespeare's works, 1623. The Felton portrait, which exhibits finer lines than that of Droeshout, has often been reproduced by engraving, first and best in 1794 by T. Trotter, from whose plate this frontispiece is made. The original painting has apparently been long since lost.

THE FELTON PORTRAIT OF SHAKESPEARE

SHAKESPEARE AND "DEMI-SCIENCE"

Papers on Elizabethan Topics

BY

FELIX E. SCHELLING

Professor in the University of Pennsylvania

PRESS OF THE UNIVERSITY OF
PENNSYLVANIA : PHILADELPHIA

1927

Reprinted from the edition of 1927, Philadelphia
First AMS EDITION published 1971
Manufactured in the United States of America

International Standard Book Number: 0-404-05585-0

Library of Congress Number: 75-126687

AMS PRESS INC.
NEW YORK, N.Y. 10003

CONTENTS

THE following papers comprise articles, reviews and addresses, variously written or delivered in the course of a long teaching career. None of them is class-room matter; several have already appeared in print; and some of these have been slightly reordered. While nothing in the nature of unity, much less continuity, can be claimed for such a collection, Shakespeare in his age dominates the volume. It is to be hoped that a certain variety in mood may not be found altogether inappropriate to the consideration of a period in which, more than in any other, comedy often trod on dignity's train and ermine.

I

SHAKESPEARE AND "DEMI-SCIENCE"

THAT SHAKESPEARE often consorts with strange companions is less an observation than a truism: for many strange people interest themselves in Shakespeare and many more of them are interested in "demi-science," a delightful term, descriptive of a dreadful thing, cleverly coined by that able wit and competent scholar, Professor Paul Shorey of the University of Chicago.[1] The reader may perhaps have noticed that our English prefix "demi" is really a very disreputable particle. It has a tendency to lower the tone and belittle the character of any work with which it has anything to do. Without the impertinence here of illustration, I am solicitous that the reader shall attach to the word "demi-science" the very worst significance that he possibly can; and instead of defining it, I shall leave the matter to his individual innocency or acquaintance with the world. For true science I have a respect, an admiration and a veneration that will yield to none. True science constitutes the most trustworthy pledge of the world's onward progress, a safeguard and a stay in the midst of much

---

[1] "The Case for the Classics," *University of Michigan Publications, Humanistic Studies*, 1910, p. 316.

that is crumbling about us. But this is science, not "demi-science." "Demi-science" is, as they put it in France, quite another affair.

With respect to our other word, "Shakespeare" means many different things to many different people. Some are not quite sure whether Shakespeare was actually a man or merely a book; others question if he ever had a name and was not rather a trust or a syndicate. One devoutly believes that, like his own Caesar, Shakespeare can do no wrong; another delights to malign him as illiterate and debauched. In a trite, old-fashioned way, I believe that Shakespeare was an actual man who once trod this planet much as other men have trod it. Peradventure he, too, knew the primrose ways: there was little in which he remained inexperienced. But that he trod in these ways to perdition of body or of soul, I find nor jot nor tittle of evidence to show. In an equally old-fashioned way, I believe that Shakespeare wrote his own works, or at least made personally his own by the divine right of his genius, the substantial body of plays that go under his name. And I recognize that however his inequality, his inconsistencies, his carelessness and peccadilloes, literary and other, may irritate precisians, Fabian philosophers and people possessed with a mission to reform art and society, Shakespeare still remains the supreme dramatic poet of the world.

Some dozen years ago, in a university summer school, situated wherever you will, east or west, a certain course begot, as was its purpose, an excellent crop of papers concerning Shakespeare and his times, the work of as earnest, eager and active a group of students as it has ever been the writer's pleasure personally to know. With one word, however, this group was obsessed; and that word was the word "psychology." They brought it to college with them every morning and cherished and coddled it all day. They played with it and worked with it; they wrestled with it as did Tobias with the angel. Psychology as a word tangled up their history and their arithmetic and imperilled what they called their "results." While as to their papers, there was scarcely one of them which was not deep, dark, prying, scientifical, and oh! how we loved that blessed word "research." To mention only one or two of our topics, there was a paper on the psychology of senile dementia as exemplified in *King Lear;* another purported to be an inquiry into the psychology of somnambulistic remorse as exhibited by Lady Macbeth. Othello and Iago prompted an investigation into the psychology of racial antipathy with anthropological parallels; and *Antony and Cleopatra* became an inquisition into the psychology of infatuation as exemplified in certain elderly and none too respectable historical personages. At last I groaned aloud; and made a little bargain with my friends and students: That we should banish the word "psychology" from our vocabulary. This agreement we faithfully kept; and it is astonishing how well we got on without it.

Psychology, I have observed, is both a science and a "demi-science." In its more reputable vocation doubtless it has its place; I cannot tell what that place

3

is, because I am not a psychologist. But I am troubled with grave doubts as to whether psychology even, is *in* place in *all* places. Almost any considerable list of recent books and articles on Shakespeare or anything else will furnish learned discussions of pseudo-scientific topics almost as absurd as those which I have alleged of my sometime students. At times it is the psychology, the psycho-analytics or rather the criminology, of the poet's own life that is pondered; and we learn that the moral wreck of a great nature, a man dying of vice and premature old age induced by a bad life, was the price that the world has paid for the works of its greatest dramatist.[2] A learned foreigner studies " abnormal personages in dramatic literature," [3] grouping Shakespeare with Ibsen and Gerard Hauptmann; while a third finds in Schopenhauer, Hamlet and Mephistopheles, to wit, a discontented philosopher, a malevolent devil of theological invention and a melancholy personage of fiction, the means of an elaborate contribution to what he calls the " natural history of pessimism." [4]

In one place we learn that Macbeth is a congenital criminal, discoverable, if we are to know him scientifically, only in the light of deep and protracted criminological investigations. Elsewhere we are told that Hamlet is paranoiac, subject to homicidal outbreaks, and that his irresolution is referable to a motive in which is involved a feature of the story of Œdipus, too

[2] T. Harris. *The Man Shakespeare and his Tragic Life.*
[3] W. Weygandt. *Abnormal Caraktere*, Hamburg, 1910.
[4] T. Paulsen. *Schopenhauer, Hamlet, Mephistophile*, Stuttgart, 1911.

4

shameful to repeat, except in the technical obscurantism of the alienist.[5] The interpretations of demi-science are both like and unlike mathematics. Both deal in figures. Mathematics deals in signs or figures which stand definitely and invariably for a given quantity, the manipulation of such figures according to rule giving definite and predicable results. Demi-science deals in figures of speech which stand now for one thing and now for another. Demi-science deals in intangibles incapable of agreement as to definition or even as to variability other than that of a difference of opinion, but most capable of a manipulation into nearly anything figurative, imaginary, new and very strange. However, my business is not with science or even with demi-science in its applications to existent humanity, whether its function be to prove the majority of mankind morons or sane, criminals unaccountable for their acts or investigators unaccountable for their theories. I am concerned here only with the interpretations which a false application of science is making us daily in the interpretation of works of art on the assumed and wholly gratuitous assumption that its pronouncements as to that abstraction, the biological man, are equally applicable to that other abstraction, the imaginative creation of the poet's brain.

Will the reader forgive me, if I suggest that one of the most absorbingly interesting themes of modern pseudo-science is that of the eternal difference of man

[5] E. Jones, "The Œdipus Complex," *American Journal of Psychology*, xxi. 72.

and woman; just as the eternal differences of men and women constitute the chief topics of our novels and our plays. A decadent poet in decadent Munich, not so very long since, told over again the story of Adam and Eve, and fitted it — perhaps it is best not to ask just how — to the modern German stage! There are four figures: Cain and Abel, now grown; Adam, waxing old and much preoccupied in gardening; Eve, the eternal feminine, who is much younger, pretty, idle and spoiling for something to do. She flirts with both her sons — there was nobody else for her to flirt with, poor dear lady — and the unhappy boys taking the matter seriously, Cain slays Abel.

The psychological interpretation of dramatic works of art, especially those of the past is apt to prove a dangerous weapon. It cuts in more ways than one. For the dramatic psycho-analyst assumes that these personages of some two hours' traffic with the stage are human beings of today, possessed of a past which he reconstructs after his own sweet will, and of a future which agnostically he has long since ceased to believe is damnation. He applies to these images of stage illusion the rigorous measurements that we habitually apply — and misapply — to actual men and women. And when his " scientific standards " fail — as fail they must — he concludes that we have in these plays of an elder age precisely the false psychology that one might expect of a self-taught, unscientific playwright; and he deplores Shakespeare's defective art and the glamour which it still seems to possess for benighted, unscientific readers.[6] One wonders whether the thumb-marks of Iago would have disclosed him a villain according to the Bertillon system, or whether, after all, it might not be more pertinent to ask, after a method more conservatively orthodox, for the imprint of Iago's foot.

Let me remark, parenthetically, that although now quite out of date, Zola remains the notorious example of an author who " shadowed the criminal mind as the detective shadows the criminal," dragging him into the police report, if perhaps not always into literature. Zola, much like his great Russian follower, Dostoiefsky, is marvellously true to the observed trivial fact, and often unaware of its triviality and want of artistic significance. He is full of reality; but no true realist; because he is concerned, not with life in the rule, but with life in the moral exception. Zola was much read in his day; but I do not think he was read for his facts, much less for his art; and there are other things that an author is read for. So, too, the more recent melodramatic hero of Italian Chauvinism, D'Annunzio, with all his merits, is scarcely read for his criminologist's truth alone. The ways of our kind are dear to us, especially their primrose ways. If, changing quite our point of view, there is anyone who really has preferred, let us say the dismal dramatic despair of Strindberg, or who now prefers such realities or unrealities as our second-rate contemporary stage or our third-

---

[6] E. E. Stoll, " Criminals in Shakespeare," *Modern Philology*, July, 1912.

rate movies afford him to our old drama's hopeful, honest and open-hearted picture of life, we can only say, making allowances for modernity, that it is a matter of taste, if it be not a matter of the want of it. Of course we cannot read Shakespeare all the time, and there are plenty of other admirable things to read, both new and old. I have seen people leave Shakespeare for a catalogue of fertilizers or a comic supplement. But it would be unfair to judge a man's religion from the circumstance that he passed the church door on a fair May morning, or his politics, from the accident that it was too wet for him to get out to vote.

It has been cleverly remarked that "the man Lord Byron tried to be was the invention of Mrs. Radcliffe," Mrs. Radcliffe, the ladylike compiler of Georgian penny-dreadfuls, or rather, to be more accurate, of guinea-terribles, those ghastly, ghostly novels of much ado about nothing whatever. By this token, is it not conceivable that the ideal man of this, that or another age, the Chevalier Bayard, the Sidney, Beau Brummel or Beau Nash, each of his time, may have exercised an appreciable influence on what his fellows tried to be? Is it not equally conceivable, too, that an ideal such as that of Castiglione's *Courtier*, its English imitation, *Euphues*, or that bugaboo, a Prince according to Machiavelli, may have exerted a palpable influence on the age in which each was popular? So that a man tried to be in turn the complete gentleman, the complete fop, or the complete villain according to his taste or proclivity? Man is a mimetic animal; indeed human mimicry is almost the best argument in favor of our simian ancestry. How well I remember how, many years ago, the excellent " grey poet," Walt Whitman, had a satellite who revolved incessantly in his orbit in a state of admiring mimicry. The poet Whitman was a large man, deliberate, not to say somewhat elephantine in his motions, partly through age. He had a splendid shock of long white hair and a beard as shaggy and noble as King Lear's. He affected ample white or grey clothing, a huge grey hat, and carried a heavy cane which his faltering steps needed. The satellite was not nearly so big, so he made it up in the looseness of his coat and in the bagginess of his trousers, to say nothing of his hat, which was enormous. He did what he could with his hair and beard, neither of which was of quite the right texture or color; and, although he was naturally brisk of movement, he affected a slow and stately step, a deliberate form of speech and, if you addressed him as " Mr. Whitman " (which we young wags sometimes did), he would love you for a week. I repeat that man is a mimetic animal. And we mimic, be it remarked, not each other's physiological psychology, but each other's manners, gait, conduct, ideals and religion. Calvinism and Machiavellism were strong enough respectively in Shakespeare's days to make men saints and sinners after a model undiscoverable in times when such ideals no longer rule the hopes and fears of men. The writers of an age that knew such saints and sinners naturally preferred a transfer of their visible traits to their poetry and drama rather than the hazardous experiment of trying to guess what the pseudo-psychologists of the twentieth century would be likely to approve or disapprove.

Another effort of " demi-science," applied to Shakespeare, is the endeavor to show how false was Shakespeare's idea of sin, evil and temptation. Mediaeval Christianity — perhaps I had better call it mediaeval Christian mythology — conceived of the world as existing as a species of bone of contention between the powers of good and evil, as a species of sketch in black and white, the raiment respectively of the legions of light and the legions of darkness, in eternal conflict for the soul of man. Still again, the mediaeval idea conceived of sin as a species of supernatural microbe, only bigger and uglier than our microscopic microbe, against which the righteous man is immune, but to whose insidious attacks the morally weak are all too liable. Now all this is very well; but does it follow that Shakespeare, the most modern of our old writers, was really governed by these notions, half of them well worn and tattered by his time? It is assuming much to affirm that all of these creations of the poet are governed by the old conception of crime as a concrete possession of the devil. Could we conceive of such a fate as Othello's and Desdemona's as wholly dependent on the machinations of Iago? Is it not what Iago's lucid tongue calls, " a frail vow betwixt an erring barbarian and a super-subtle Venetian " and their defiance of social forces that discountenance such ill-assorted marriages, that make all Iago's plotting possible?

To Macbeth much attention is devoted by this devotee of the new science, to show in him a state of "unrepentant horror" which the critic finds not in the modern villain. But assuredly Macbeth is a being not so monstrous and unaccountable even in the categories of modern science. Waving the inconsistency, already pointed out, of the comparison of a person of the imagination with an actual being, two points may here be urged, the ineptitude of judging the old age by ours, and the unhappiness of the assumption that these protagonists who become criminal by passion (as in Othello) or because of opportunity (as in Macbeth), by accident, or the malignity of Fate (as in Romeo), are congenital criminals of the type that sets them apart from the rest of mankind. May not an age that accepted the dualism of mediaeval mythology have bred just such unstable, imaginative, and remorseless villains as Macbeth, whether Signor Lombroso met a counterpart in the prisons of Milan or not? And if Macbeth, Iago, and Edmund were the congenital criminals of modern science, an imperfect group of maimed humanity with the stigmata of crime upon them, could Shakespeare, or anybody else, have made plays about them? Into the details of the deeper Freudian "subterranean psychology" with its psychoanalyses of the subliminal consciousness, I may not be too wise, but I am much too wary, to enter. These things concern the student of literature only in so far as their extravagances affect and bias the scholarship of zealous but imprudent men.

It is scarcely a generation since perfections in the art of photography began to make themselves felt in our current illustration. Indubitably the ordinary illustrator of today can draw something rather more close to the actual position of a galloping horse, than the usual illustrator of forty years ago. Science may correct imperfect, undeveloped, or faulty art; but had the old masters a real need of the camera? And does great art, or any art worthy the name, consist in mere anatomical correctness? Michelangelo knew too much about anatomy, not too little; and it was Andrea del Sarto who could set right the faulty drawing of Raphael, to remain only Andrea del Sarto thereafter. Art is the representation of things, men, emotions, and passions seen in an atmosphere. Science is the contemplation of things in an unbiassed, unemotional, unincumbered vacuum. This is why the naturalist novels of Zola, the pessimist's psychology of Ibsen, and most of the delightfully capable, mechante and absolutely unrealistic earlier comedies of the admirable Mr. Shaw have already proved ephemeral. They substituted, each in his own degree, the rationalized processes of science, which distinguish and divide, for the emotional processes of art, which are synthetical and harmonizing. They give us negation where art demands affirmation. They remain temporary where art is eternal. Wherefore all are already hull-down on the horizon.

We talk glibly of going back to nature, and some people know of no nature except the overdone cult of green fields and out of doors; as if a vegetable, a cabbage or a violet, had in it more of nature than that marvellous complexity of beast and god, of earth, flesh, devil and spirit that we call a man. All art is conventional and limited by the medium in which it works. In picture we agree to accept two dimensions, retaining color, light and perspective to simulate the third. In statuary, for the most part, we eschew color and permit the convention of bronze or marble to simulate the color of human flesh and its covering raiment. In poetry we commonly accept rhythm, rime, choice of epithets, and figures of speech to symbolize the heightened mental excitement in which the spirit of poetry lives and has its being; and in drama equally we heighten at once the similitude of the scene and raise it to higher terms than those of life by a selection, out of the seething caldron of actual existence, of those passions, those situations, and personages that most logically and most completely represent the phase of human activity and story which has been chosen. Few men in actual life, save lunatics, talk aloud to themselves; no man, except a coxcomb, addresses his beloved in rime or even in blank-verse; — shall we therefore conclude that Hamlet's insanity is established, and that Romeo's passion for Juliet was as affected as his puppy-love for the "unexpressive Rosaline?" Art is not life, and life is not art. As Professor Bradley has so well put it, the two are parallel and ever related, but actually never touching; and to judge either alone by the standards of the other is to fall into confusion.[7] It is undeniable that all human activities are governed by the sanction of prec-

[7] A. C. Bradley, "Poetry for Poetry's Sake," *Oxford Lectures on Poetry*, 1911.

13

edent, and that we need the rebel in art, politics and religion, to call us from the ridiculous perpetuation of the eternal human game of follow-my-leader. But let us trust to the seer, if it is our religion that is to be reformed, to the statesman, if the cry is for wider, truer liberty; and to the poet, if we are to establish once more the divinity of art.

Now let us turn back to Shakespeare, this time without " demi-science." Shakespeare is not perfect. I like to think of him, not as the least of the demigods — that removes him away from human kind — but as the greatest of human artists, sharing the ways of his fellowmen and loving them as we know that he loved them. Shakespeare is the most contemporaneous of authors. He translates everything into the vivid terms of his own present; and he saw that present not in one of its aspects, but in all. Shakespeare introduces you to higher life than you have been accustomed to and to lower life than you like to associate with. And all of it he saw without tremor and unafraid.

When great men die in Shakespeare's plays, portents foretell their falls. Strange things happened in the streets of Rome the night before Caesar was murdered; stranger wonders portend the dire results of the witches' tampering with the murderous impulses of Macbeth. Now all this Shakespeare found in his sources and, following them, he set the flood, the comets, the carnivorous horses, and the monstrous births, all faithfully down. This was a part of the life and the belief of his time, to omit it was to be psychologically as well as historically and poetically untrue.

But mark, in *King Lear*, it is the easy-going elderly Gloster who believes in portents and signs of impending disaster; his wicked son, Edmund, ridicules such things in the spirit of atheistical unbelief; and we jump to the conclusion that Shakespeare was not only a man of faith but a superstitious man who associated a disbelief in witchcraft with a disbelief in God. But how hasty we are. There is a charming familiar passage in *A Midsummer Night's Dream* — cut out usually on the modern stage as too lengthy. It tells of the dreadful effects of an inverted year, of floods, desolated country, dying flocks and general rural disaster, and *all* because Titania, that mite of a fairy queen, has quarrelled with Oberon, her fairy husband. Here is the passage which will give you Shakespeare's own ideas of comets, portents and the like. He is laughing at you over his little pigmies, the fairies, and wondering if we human pigmies are any bigger, any wiser, any less hopelessly self-centered.

Take Shakespeare's treatment of the mob which has been much censured by sociologists. He wrote, be it remembered, long before books on the psychology of the crowd had been invented, so pity his ignorant plight. Shakespeare does not like man huddled together in masses; he has none of the slum-worker's yearning for the submerged tenth. He has observed — and that without the help of statistics — that crowds are commonly noisy, dirty, liable to do things, even to perpetrate crimes, that hardly any individual among them would dare. And he stands off from that sort of thing and rallies the brainlessness of the mob and its fickleness.[8] He probably never formulated such an idea: but he would have recognized that the history of man is made up of a series of triumphs of the minority over the majority. And he might have been so undemocratic as to question whether all things, sacred and mundane, are safely to be decided by a show of hands. He would have recognized that art at least cares nothing for dull averages, for the man in the street *as* the man in the street, but that it is the individual traits that count, not necessarily those of station, but those that indicate the actual man within. We object to Shakespeare's representation of watchmen, servants and other common folk as stupid, vulgar and futile; is stupidity, vulgarity and futility, even in our own day, the exclusive privilege of the well born? And do we pay no deference to the rich, the titled or the powerful? Shakespeare saw his world steadily, far more steadily, we may surmise, than we habitually see ours or than " demi-science " sees it for us.

The most foolish of books is a book of sentiments and quotations, culled from their context and labelled Shakespeare's. We exclaim " Ah, the universal poet! how wise he is! " " Put money in thy purse." " Neither a borrower nor a lender be." What a worldly-wise old fellow is this! But who said " Put money in thy purse " ? Iago, not Shakespeare. And who said " Neither a borrower nor a lender be " ? Why, a " tedious old fool," named Polonius. No passage of Shake-

[8] See F. Tupper, " The Shakespeare Mob," *Modern Language Publications*, xxvii.

peare, or any veritable dramatist, for that matter, is safe quoted for itself and out of its context. In this kaleidoscopic thing which we call a world, it is never safe to stop and palter over a single broken bit of colored glass. In its place it bears a relation to the pattern of the whole; out of place, it is nothing. Shakespeare saw not only steadily, he saw the world as a whole.

Shakespeare's world was not our world. We do not wear ruffs or farthingales, we do not strike our servants, — we haven't any to strike and when we have they do the striking. We do not chop off the heads of our traitors; and we do not believe in God as fervently as the Elizabethans believed in the devil. But these things are in a sense superficial. In a deeper sense, Shakespeare's world was much the world we live in and it will remain such. For in that imaginary world of his, truth, honor, lofty ideals, hope for the future and respect for the past stand as high as the tiniest moralist of us all has ever been able to reach up and place them. Have you ever met two as gallant young gentlemen as Harry Monmouth and Hotspur? Have you ever known as witty and fascinating a rogue as Falstaff; as bewitching a maiden as Rosalind, as adorable a woman as Imogen? These true personages are easier to accept and believe in, easier to understand as alive and breathing than half the historical personages whose existence on this planet can be proved by the evidence of documents. No scientist could compose them, no statistician juggle them together, no criminologist compass their incomparable perfections by an excursus into their opposite deviations. The poet has breathed his soul into them and they are immortal.

And here let us take leave of Shakespeare and all the " demi-sciences." To be wise in his own generation is the dearest of the follies of man; and perhaps I have drawn up much unnecessary artillery in this case to the demolition of a molehill. Scholarship waxes in its pride, and wanes; and out of its overtoppled towers and ruined battlements of strength new and wiser scholarship arises. Of one thing alone are we certain: Above all this petty turmoil and stirring of the lower air, the greatest poet rears his head as serene and unperturbed as the Sphinx, and in some respects as unfathomable, secure against the little hurricanes of sand that may temporarily bury his feet, eternally triumphant in the imperishability of his art.

II

MYTH MAKING

A WELL KNOWN TEACHER of homiletics — less learnedly, sermon making — burst into a group of his friends one day with the remark: "My reputation is gone, and a trial for heresy is in order." As he was a clergyman as notable for his piety as for his learning, we expressed our amazement and inquired into the theological point of his unorthodoxy. "I have failed," he replied, "to fix the geographical spot in which the prodigal son shared his husks with the swine. I do not know whether he traveled east or west to the home of his father. I do not know to which of the ten tribes of Israel this interesting family belonged. And I have even questioned the existence, before the feast, of the fatted calf." Our friend had been explaining that the famous parable was a myth, not an historical occurrence; and his class, which had doubtless been carefully innoculated in the Kindergarten with rationalistic views as to Santa Claus, in horror detected a question as to the stated facts, the authenticity of the Bible.

It seems that Professor Abel Lefranc, of the College de France, has elaborated a theory whereby Shakespeare is once more deprived of authorship in his own plays and they are handed over, this time, to William Stanley, the sixth Earl of Derby.[1] This earl, like everybody else in his time, was interested in the drama and, like nearly every other earl, was the patron of a theatrical company. There is even a report among the State Papers that, about the time that *As You Like It* was on the stage, Derby was "busied only in penning comedies for the common players." These are the grounds upon which Professor Lefranc has reared his speculative buttresses, an uncommonly flimsy one among them being the statement that no other Englishman of that age could have given us scenes so French — save the mark — as those of *Love's Labour's Lost*. But it is not this that is interesting.

Professor Lefranc, it may be observed, is an eminent authority on Rabelais. It is always an eminent authority on something else who makes new and startling discoveries concerning Shakespeare. Now it is an eminent jurist, or a novelist; anon, it is a scientist or a reporter or a spiritualist. There is something about actual knowledge — even a little of it — as to Shakespeare and his times, which precludes the making of startling discoveries by anybody but an eminent specialist in something else. Wherefore it was reserved for a publisher of books to find one of the dozen or more ciphers elucidating one of the dozen or more "mysteries" as to the authorship of Shakespearean plays; and to a madwoman to suspect that "the whole secret" was hidden away with the poet's bones in Stratford Church. It was an American doctor who "digged"

[1] A. Lefranc, *Sous le Masque de Shakespeare*, 1919.

in the ford of an English river to find a casket holding "the mystery" of this authorship, doubtless very completely in solution. And it was a British barrister who discovered that the man who wrote these plays likewise penned the bulk of Elizabethan literature. Our heart goes out to this last poor devil, chained to his desk eternally to write from early morn to dewy eve, at a low estimate as to mere penmanship for at least fifty arduous years. Hail immortal Tom, Francis or Billy the Penman!

Now which of us knows an unadulterated fact when face to face with it? And will the huddling of any number of facts in one brain inform, educate or improve in any wise its unhappy possessor? Facts are nothing until ordered and correlated into that substance of a higher order which we call truth. And facts are as helpful — if that be the word — to the building of a fabric of falsehood. It is, according to some who profess to know, a fact that Washington was a fox-hunting squire, that he owned and occasionally whipped slaves and that his personal morality was much that of his time. More of such facts, not a hundred like them, could account for this particular fox-hunting squire, who was likewise a patriot, a general of indomitable spirit, a statesman controlling the trend of history and guiding the destiny of a great nation. The favorite myth of the hatchet and the cherry tree may be rationally demolished with ease. Was it a cherry tree? Or a pear? Was there a tree? Perhaps the hatchet was actually that handier implement, an ax. Was there even an ax? But what of all these facts? The truth lies in the parable; the integrity of the boy "who could not tell a lie" was the integrity of the man who founded an empire.

Once more, I understand that the researches of historians disprove the fine old story that Jefferson, upon his inauguration to the presidency, rode up alone to the capitol on a white horse, tied him to a post, took the oath of office, and rode as simply and unattended home again. The horse, it is said, was really not white, there were actually two of him, harnessed to a livery stable carriage and attended as usual by other horses similarly hired and harnessed to other equipages. But what, again, of all these proofs? The myth remains an admirably true designation of Jeffersonian simplicity; and no accumulation of mere proofs and disproofs could so create the atmosphere of truth.

The Psalmist was possibly more discourteous than untruthful in his outburst: "I said in my heart all men are liars," as even the least accomplished among us find it less difficult to draw a long bow than a nice line of distinction between what we are sure of and what we are not so certain about. Myth-making is an equal strain on human ingenuity and human honesty; but to neither is it wholly discreditable. And it is ultimately referable to the artist, innate in us all. If we are able to tell stories — and pray, sir, who among us does not tell stories — why not tell them well? And what true artist has ever been hampered by life studies in the poses of a naked fact?

Greatness is inherent: but fame is recognition of greatness or the report of greatness. The greater the fame, therefore, the richer the myth. Babes, in further Asia on their mother's knees, are stilled, even now, with folk-tales of Alexander of Macedon, and the horrors of the Attila of a heightened fiction have only been equalled by the realities made in Germany in our own times. There is no saint, canonized or potential, who does not attract to himself the nimbus of a glory not his own. And there is no merely human creature whose fellows do not contrive, humanly or inhumanly, to gossip about him, to magnify or minimize him. Whenever popular esteem has gathered repute about a man so that he becomes a Marcus Aurelius, let us say, or a King Arthur, there are always the diggers in the dust-bins of time to disprove his virtues or perhaps his existence. And whenever the popular imagination has found in some portentous figure, such as Richard Crookback or Benedict Arnold, an object of abhorrence and revolt, there is always some casuist at hand to show that he was, after all, a very reputable citizen. The whitewashing of great scoundrels is one of the most approved and elegant pursuits of the modern historian. And the contemporary art of maligning and blackening great names is by no means wholly lost among us. Thus are we always raveling and unraveling our myths, tearing the fabrics of the past to weave them anew into novel designs and in striking and bizarre colors.

The greater the repute, then, the richer the myth; for a larger corps of myth-makers are at work; and unfortunate is he about whom no one of his fellow men has anything to fabricate. Few of us escape being thought something other than we are; and this, for the most part, is fortunate; for, when all is said, myth balances myth and such an airy habitation as has been made for many a man is often quite as good as a name. An honest myth is the noblest work of man; and man and nation is inevitably to be appraised by the myth he makes. When a reportorial person finds out to his own satisfaction, as one such did a few years ago, that Shakespeare was the Oscar Wilde of his time, a man of an utterly base and debauched life, and that the price which the world had to pay for the greatest of plays was the wreck of the greatest of personalities, we may not know what to make of such a Shakespeare, but we know exactly what to make of the reportorial person aforesaid. When another writer, posing as a detective, scents fraud and deception in every unsuspected act of an author's life, and a malign and covert allusiveness in every other harmless passage of his poetry, we know just what to think of a nature so petty and prying. Depend upon it by their myths ye shall know them, for there is nothing so infallibly a man's own as the myth that he fashions.

None the less, if we view the thing aright there are few things more creditable to human nature than this tendency to turn everything into myth; for the process is essentially a quest after truth. It is the great popular figures of history, literature and art about which myth most readily gathers — Alexander, Cleopatra, Barbarossa, Shakespeare, Beethoven — for there are thousands building up, each for himself, his contribution to the conception of truth. Facts, as such, are things thought of theoretically. Truth gives us the world in its interrelations, things seen in atmosphere. Nothing exists in a vacuum — not even the man of fact — although one would fain wish sometimes that he did. Wherefore atmosphere is essential if we are to get at reality. There is no scientific fact which can pass from mind to mind without some generalization into truth, some play of the imagination in the process. The making of myths is the breaking loose of the creative impulses and creation, according to the true idea, is the basis of all the arts. Let us keep our myths in the interests of truth as in the interests of beauty.

III

THE SEEDPOD OF SHAKESPEARE
CRITICISM

THE SUGGESTION, the kernel of this title is
that most obvious of disparities, the difference
between an acorn and an oak. Though if the origins
of comment on Shakespeare and his work are to be
likened to an acorn, we shall have to find something
more tangled, confused and impenetrable, something
less dignified than an oak, properly to figure forth that
dense, overgrown and fanciful jungle, Shakespeare
criticism. Paths there are few through it, and these
are wandering and zig zag. Much of its growth is like
the upas tree, sprouting upward to impede and down-
ward to entangle, illogical, presumptuous, unnecessary, a good deal of it, and uninformed. Yet all these
fronds and dangling vines, with some sound growth
as well, have sprung from some seed and as we follow
back in imagination we come closer and closer to the
simple beginnings whence it has all come.

Many years ago, when bicycles were in vogue, I was
captured, one fine summer day, by a sometime student
of mine who was then the president of a freshwater
college up the state. Small clothes and all, I was carried into a big auditorium to talk, on a few moments'

notice; and I asked for any copy of Shakespeare that
might be at hand. I had in mind that prefatory material to the first folio of the plays about which everybody knows and which few people have ever read.
Though possessed of numerous editions of Shakespeare, not one book could be found in that college
which reprinted this ancient material, and I naturally
talked about something else. Later, investigating the
matter, I realized that this introductory material of the
old folio is seldom if ever reprinted in modern editions
of Shakespeare, as every editor is anxious to write
something prefatory of his own. We could perhaps
spare the dedication " To the most noble and incomparable pair of brethren, William Earl of Pembroke,
etc., Lord Chamberlain to the King's most excellent
majesty, and Philip, Earl of Montgomery, etc., gentleman of his majesty's bedchamber, both knights of the
most noble order of the garter and our singular good
lords." It is admirably written in the eulogistic manner of the time, which, like its towering ruffs, its em-
broidered and brocaded jerkins and stomachers and
farthingales, elaborately concealed much of the real
men and women beneath. But can we spare from the
book that reprints the words of Hamlet, Falstaff and
Imogen, the vivacious preface, " To the great variety
of readers," an address which includes everyone of
us, " from the more able (which means you of course,
dear reader), to him who can but spell? " Can we
spare the fine lines " To the memory of my beloved,
the author, Master William Shakespeare and what he
hath left us," penned by the greatest poet, dramatic or

other, who survived Shakespeare in his day? Even the lesser praises of two or three minor men are not impertinent, to say nothing of the Droeshout portrait of the title page and Jonson's epigram about it "To the Reader." When my friend, then Professor Neilson of Harvard, now president of Smith College, yielded to the blandishments of a publisher and edited *The Complete Works of Shakespeare*, exceedingly well but printed in that wicked wise, the double column, I expostulated with him for this omission, which long since he has corrected; and now at least in one modern edition we may read our Shakespeare as he came from the press and find these opening passages which, albeit his pen did not trace them, are yet as veritably a part of his book as Marc Antony's address to the populace of Rome over the body of the dead Caesar or as the sleep-walking scene in *Macbeth*.

A book, handed down for generations without its true title, without dedication, preface or recommendadation, can we wonder that "seeliest Ignorance" has found something suspiciously irregular in such a publication of Shakespeare's works? I will not say that Baconianism and other like nonsense is founded on that omission, for Baconianism is prodigenously learned, if in the wrong way. But it is not to be questioned that we have lost much of the historical atmosphere of this most important book by this particular sin of omission, and by our editorial disregard of the apparatus with which the famous volume was first issued to the world.

Now if there is anything concerning Shakespeare

about which we may be permitted to be certain, it is
the circumstance that there is absolutely no mystery
about the publication of his plays. All the mysteries
about him, indeed, are of our own making. Shakespeare's collected works — for with these alone are we
now concerned — were published seven years after his
death, (a remarkably early publication), under conditions so simple, so obvious, so understandable that
anyone, knowing the practices of the time as to publication, could have predicted them, one and all. May
I epitomize the old story? Shakespeare died in 1616,
the second member — that is the second largest stock-
holder — in a theatrical company which may be described as Burbage, Shakespeare, Heminge and Company; and another player, named Condell, was the
treasurer of the firm. Burbage, greatest actor of the
age, followed Shakespeare to the grave in 1619; whereupon the firm name might be read as Heminge, Condell and Company. Today, when a merchant dies,
his heirs inherit his stock in trade in the firm. In
Shakespeare's day, such property was often appor-
tioned among the surviving members of the firm or
company. Wherefore all the plays which Shakespeare
had written for his company, the King's Men, became
vested in Heminge and Condell. Now turn to the
modernly omitted prefatory material of the famous
first folio and you will find both the dedication and the
the address " to the great variety of readers " signed
" John Heminge and Henry Condell," for they with
their fellows were as veritably the owners of the plays
of their company which were as yet unprinted, as they

were the veritable owners of the Theater on the Bankside and their other house in Blackfriars.

But the plays as yet printed were by no means all of them. In Shakespeare's time there was no such thing as a copyright. The booksellers had adopted an arrangement in the Stationers' — that is Booksellers' — Register, by which they protected themselves against each other. A phrase of the day was " escaped into print," and when a book had once " escaped into print," its own author had no warrant in law or in equity to claim it. About half of Shakespeare's plays were printed in his lifetime, sometimes in the first instance against his and his company's will, though often, we may well believe, with permission, and even in rivalry with the " stolen and surreptitious copies." More of Shakespeare's plays were printed within his lifetime and in a greater number of editions than the plays of any other playwright; and for the simple reason that the Elizabethans appreciated Shakespeare above all other men who wrote for the stage and liked to read him as well as to see him acted. The printed sources of the folio were owned by some eight or ten printers who had come by them variously; so to adjust the claims of all, a syndicate was formed, headed by the printers, Isaac Jaggard, the King's printer, and Edward Blount, the most prominent of contemporary booksellers, to combine with Heminge and Condell, the theatrical owners, in the collection and publication in one volume of everything which Shakespeare had written. Look now once more at the neglected prefatory material of this book, and the title page will disclose to you "Mr. William Shakespeare's Comedies, Histories and Tragedies published according to the true original copies, London, printed by Isaac Jaggard and Ed. Blount, 1623."

And now a question arose. Neither Heminge or Condell was a writer, and such a book ought to be properly introduced. In such a juncture there could be no choice. The best book of the hour demanded sponsorship by the greatest contemporary man of letters. Ben Jonson was the King's poet, the laureate, the literary dictator of the age; and Jonson rose nobly to the task, penning not only the epigram "To the Reader" and his noble personal eulogium, but both the prose addresses of dedication. Of this matter there can be no question whatsoever; the style and phraseology of both disclose the author; and if anyone is troubled by the signatures of Heminge and Condell, appended to two addresses which neither of them actually wrote, let him examine into his own conduct in the matter of circulars, resolutions, and other papers which he has had written by skilled competence for the appendage of his signature. There was no deceit in the practice and none was intended.

The famous first folio of Shakespeare is not a notable specimen of book printing. The age knew handsomer volumes and more correctly printed ones. But save for Ben Jonson's own folio of 1616 (and Jonson was a bookish man), nobody's plays had ever been collected together for print in England up to this time. The age must have thought something of these productions so to collect and publish them. It would have been a wonder if Ben Jonson had critically edited them, for nobody then did such a thing for any author save an ancient classic; and it would have been a miracle if anyone had so anticipated his age as to have prefixed any account of the author to his works. Everybody knew Will Shakespeare; why write about him? As yet it was only the author's picture, not his life, that had been taken; and the Droeshout portrait, such as it is, we have.

But we have forgotten our seedpod? By no means. We have already cracked the outer shell of it. To return, there is scarcely anything about the Elizabethan age which is more astonishing than the existence in it of so many men who were great in things which Shakespeare, with all his universality, does not touch. Leaving out of consideration Spenser, who is medieval, allegorical, metaphysical, manipulatory of scholarly and classical material, all of which Shakespeare never is, we have Hooker, Bacon and Jonson, each an intellectual giant and in a sphere, each his own and wholly alien to Shakespeare's. Hooker is the great master of church polity, formal logic and philosophic reasoning, a pure and beautiful spirit, deeply religious, even more deeply theological. Now, do you know the form of Shakespeare's religious faith? What exactly was it that he believed and disbelieved? Was he a high churchman or a low? Was he a dissenter? and from what? There were many sects in his day. An old play thus reels them off: " Papist, Protestant, Puritan, Brownist, Anabaptist, Millenary, Family o'Love, Jew,

Turk, Infidel, Atheist, Good-Fellow, etc.: "[1] was Shakespeare any of these? except the last in a sense quite untheological? You will find so much religion in him and so little theology, be it remarked, that you may perhaps take him to be of your own particular sect. He has been thought by some to have been a Roman Catholic. He venerates what is beautiful and touching in the old faith and is tender with its clergy. But to the credit of human discernment, as the late Professor Raleigh once wittily put it, as yet nobody has declared Shakespeare to have been a Puritan.

Bacon was the great questioner, the man of science and classification rather than the metaphysician; in his lesser walks in life, the lawyer, the courtier, the diplomat, moving perilously among the pitfalls and falling into one of the most despicable of them, that of bribery. It is amazing that these two men, Shakespeare and Bacon, could have been each so great in his seemingly universal sphere and yet so in contrast. Bacon was well born, superbly educated, subtly skilled in diplomacy, statecraft, and the ways of courts; critical, self-seeking, aristocratic, ambitious of worldly advancement and of fame, grasping the known sphere of human knowledge as his by prerogative of the intellect. Shakespeare was of humble birth, educated more by means of an " experiencing nature " than by schools or books; one who loved in his day both " cakes and ale " and disdained not the acquisition of "lands and beeves," but to whom there was likewise ever present

[1] *Eastward Ho*, v. 2.

a world of the fancy wherein disported Puck and Ariel, a greater realm of the imagination out of which to conceive the highest poetry than has yet come from the brain of man. Shakespeare's sphere is no less complete than Bacon's, and it is far more permanent. Shakespeare's was not the world of human knowledge with its limitations and its provisional judgments, but the world of artistry and the imagination with its illimitable range of human emotion, human passion and aspiration. To anybody possessed of the most rudimentary powers of discrimination, the confusion of these two intellectual giants, Bacon and Shakespeare, is the last conceivable of errors.

Ben Jonson offers us still another contrast. Jonson is the man of books, the scholar incarnate, the moralist, the satirist, the caricaturist at times. He sees the world with the narrowed eyes of critical scrutiny; Shakespeare with the open eyes of appreciation, wonder and loving acceptance. Jonson worships cleverness, intellect; he condones knavery and detests fools. Shakespeare cares more for our human instincts and affections, and he hates nobody. Jonson comes dangerously near at times to preaching, even in his plays; Shakespeare is ever the artist, and the artist is antithetical alike to the moralist and the critic. With Jonson criticism enters the field of English letters for the first time; and here begins the opening of our seed-pod. When I say that with Jonson criticism enters the field of English letters for the first time, I do not mean to deny the existence of much comment on men and things before Jonson's time; nor do I forget the formal attempts of schoolmasters, preachers, pedants and satirists to tell us exactly how things ought to be otherwise. But there was a new formality in Jonson, not to be found in enthusiastic books like Sidney's *Defence of Poesy,* a new attitude of mind in which a pair of scales is set up on the counter of life and nothing permitted to pass over it until tried in a balance with iron weights, and then appraised, and ticketed. It is a question perhaps if this was much of a gain to the shop. But at any rate it substituted the judicial attitude, which is that of the learned judge on the woolsack, for the simpler associations of equality. Ben Jonson is the first of our authors — though by no means the last — to assume an authority over his readers on the score of being an author. The age was accustomed enough to authority from its lords, its soldiers, its preachers; but why a man should presume to tell you what you ought to think, because, forsooth, he hath written a book — this was a new doctrine.

Jonson had an opinion about everything. Like a modern economist or " educator," you could not have surprised him unfurnished with a theory; and, unlike some of these moderns his theories were based on deep learning and tempered with experience and a judicial attitude of mind. Jonson talked criticism for forty years and his world listened admiringly, happy to be guided in opinion by so wise and clever a man. At the Mermaid Tavern, " the Sun, the Dog, the Triple Tun," later in the Apollo Room of the Devil Tavern, and at the hospitable boards of many " great ones," Jonson supplied his age with criticism of the drama, of poetry, letters, which the British public now finds in the literary columns of *The Times*, and in journals such as *The Saturday Review* or what was lately *The Athenæum*. The influence of Jonson's theory and practise of literature on his age is incapable of exaggeration. He literally dominated his time. Wherefore the importance to be attached to his opinions. Unhappily Jonson's criticism was mostly talked and only occasionally noted down as in some interesting cases which shall now claim our attention.

In 1619 Jonson, who was threatened with obesity, determined on exercise as a remedy, and set out on foot from London to Edinburgh, stopping for the most part of nights at the houses of admiring friends among the nobility and gentry. It may be surmised that his nights sometimes undid his days; for the simple Elizabethans had not yet learned of the sinfulness of thirst and practiced several methods of alleviating it "with no allaying Thames." In Edinburgh the prominent Scottish poet and laird, William Drummond, entertained Jonson for some weeks at his beautiful home, Hawthornden; and, chatting daily with him, noted the great poet's comments and personal gossip in a precious document which was left by one of his descendants to the Society of Antiquaries of Scotland and which was only printed in its completeness some 230 years after Jonson's death.[2] I should like to dwell on some of the entertaining gossip and comment of these

[2] I do not share the "doubts" lately cast on the authenticity of the celebrated *Conversations*. See C. L. Stainer, *Jonson and Drummond, a Few Remarks on an Eighteenth Century Forgery*, 1925. See P. Simpson, in *Review of English Studies*, ii. 42.

Conversations of Drummond with Jonson. How he declared that " Spenser's stanzas pleased him not, nor his matter; " that " Marston wrote his father-in-law's preachings, and his father-in-law his comedies; " that " he esteemeth John Donne the first poet in the world in some things " but that " Donne, for not keeping of accent, deserved hanging." [3] Similarly shrewd and terse are the two deliverances of the *Conversations* as to Shakespeare: one is that Shakespeare " wanted art; " the other calls attention to the absurdity of anybody's suffering shipwreck on the coast of Bohemia. Here is the critic appraising a trifle, a spot on the sun — and a spot *is* striking on the face of so bright and radiant a luminary. The old age accepted the sea-coast of Bohemia and the pistol of Pericles, the sombreros of the conspirators in *Julius Caesar* and the striking clock in republican Rome; but the new critic recoiled at these things and called them a " want of art," that is, a deficiency in artifice and attention to detail, which I am inclined to think we must confess they really are. Jonson nowhere actually criticises Shakespeare for not writing like the ancients. But Jonson himself, trying to write in a manner which should profit by ancient example and succeeding measurably well, has, from these little observations, come to be taken as the champion of classical ideals as against Shakespeare's unquestionably romantic spirit. Here is the first seed in our pod, by the happy art of generalization soon to grow into much, having to do with allegations of Shakespeare's " carelessness," his

[3] " Conversations," Gifford Cunningham, *Jonson*, vol. ix.

"want of constructive ability," (Jonson was both careful and constructive), having to do with Shakespeare's untaught genius (Jonson's genius was nothing if not abundantly taught), together with the rest of the innumerable phrases and designations of the school of critical condescension, headed by Pope and Warburton; until Shakespeare became to the former an undomesticated fowl, "warbling his native woodnotes wild," and to M. Voltaire, "a natural born savage, drunk with the wine of genius." From the abundant outpourings of the school of critical condescension we have recovered only partially in this generation of our own.

Like Dryden after him, Ben Jonson's common sense was occasionally at variance with his learning; for learning is the acquisition of an uncommon sense, rather than the maintenance of a common one. When Jonson died, a note book or a commonplace-book, as such were called, was found among his papers. In it he had noted passages of his extensive reading among the ancients, translating them into literary and well-filed English and applying them to certain persons at times. For example he begins a fine paragraph on Dominus Verulanus, whom we call without any warrant whatsoever "Lord Bacon," with these words: "Yet there happened in my time one noble speaker who was full of gravity in his speaking; his language, where he could spare or pass by a jest, was nobly censorious. No man ever spake more neatly, more presly, more weightily, or suffered less emptiness, less idleness, in what he uttered. No member of his speech

38

but consisted of his own graces. His hearers could not cough, or look aside from him, without loss. He commanded where he spoke, and had his judges angry and pleased at his devotion." [4]

Now this passage is almost word for word a transcription from Seneca the Elder, but not a plagiarism; for an ability " to convert the substance or riches of another poet to his own uses " was one of Jonson's frankly avowed requisites " in our poet," as it is and ever has been a requisite in the honorable guild of authorship. Jonson is merely refreshingly frank about it.

In *Timber, or Discoveries upon Men and Matter,* as the whole title of Jonson's commonplace-book runs, you will find much about poetry, about language, style and oratory; and besides, discourse of princes, state and other weighty subjects discussed with the brevity of table-talk and culled, a blossom here, rich fruit there, from the poet's discursive reading up and down the ages. But the most precious parts of the book are the little summaries on his contemporaries such as that on the oratory of Bacon just quoted above and the famous passage about Shakespeare, our fellow country-man, which illustrates, better than any other, Jonson's scholarly preconceptions, dashed with the lucid intervals of his robust common sense. " I remember " he says, " the players have often mentioned it as an honor to Shakespeare, that in his writing, whatsoever he penned, he never blotted out a line. My answer hath been, 'Would he had blotted a thousand,'

[4] *Discoveries,* ed. Schelling, 1892, p. 30.

which they thought a malevolent speech. I had not told posterity this but for their ignorance, who chose that circumstance to commend their friend by wherein he most faulted; and to justify mine own candor." Here speaks the scholar, the professional, the man who invests his talent, who reprobates the readiness, the spendthrift habits, he would call them, of genius. But immediately Jonson's common sense, which was quickened by a warm heart, asserts itself, and he continues: " for I loved the man, and do honor his memory on this side idolatry as much as any. He was, indeed, honest, (Jonson's favorite adjective for himself), and of an open and free nature; had an excellent fancy, brave notions, and gentle expressions." And once more the critic gets the upper hand and he concludes, balancing the judicial scales: " gentle expressions, wherein he flowed with that facility that sometime it was necessary he should be stopped. ' *Sufflaminandus erat,*' as Augustus said of Haterius. His wit was in his own power; would the rule of it had been so too. Many times he fell into those things, could not escape laughter, as when he said in the person of Caesar, one speaking to him: ' Caesar, thou dost me wrong.' He replied: ' Caesar did never wrong but with just cause: ' and such like, which were ridiculous." [5] Jonson is here alluding to the reply of Caesar to Metellus which in the text which we have reads:

> Know, Caesar doth not wrong, nor without cause
> Will he be satisfied.

[5] *Ibid.,* 23.

And it is within the range of possibility that Shakespeare had written:

> Know Caesar doth not wrong but with just cause,
> Nor without cause will he be satisfied,

and that he altered the passage, leaving the line imperfect, in a deference to Jonson's criticism; although he may well have meant by " doth not wrong," " do no injury " in which case Jonson's criticism loses all its point. However, be it remembered that Jonson did not publish this criticism. He concludes, " but he redeemed his vices with his virtues. There was ever more in him to be praised than to be pardoned." Here is another seed of our pod: Shakespeare allowed with judicial qualification and allowance, the critical attitude of Dr. Johnson and the rout of writers who followed him and are marching in his track contentedly to the present day.

But let us turn back now to the prefatory material of the folio with which we began. The epigram facing " this figure that . . . was for gentle Shakespeare cut " gives us, besides the appropriate accolade of a true gentility in the famous designation " the gentle Shakespeare," the notable advice: " Reader, look not on his picture but his book." It were good for us if we followed this advice more often instead of reading — even as now, alas — so much about Shakespeare. " To the great variety of readers " addressing us personally, numbering us, in Jonsonian wise, according to our wits and capacities to acquire for ourselves a cheap Shakespeare or a dear Shakespeare (and some of our Shakespeares are woefully cheap); and "then" continues Jonson, "judge your six-pen'orth, your shilling's worth, your five shillings' worth at a time (according to your divers capacities) . . . but, whatever you do, buy." " For," he adds in splendid affirmation of Shakespeare's enthusiastic acceptance by his own age: " know, these plays have had their trial already and stood out all appeals; and do now come forth quitted rather by a decree of court than any purchased letters of commendation." Then comes the regret which has echoed down the ages: " It had been a thing, we confess, worthy to have been wished that the author himself had lived to have set forth and overseen his own writings; " and the tribute to his facility as " a happy imitator of nature, . . . and a most gentle expresser of it. His mind and hand went together: and what he thought, he uttered with that easiness that we have scarce received from him a blot in his papers. . . . And there we hope to your divers capacities, you will find enough, both to draw, and hold you: for his wit can no more lie hid, than it could be lost. Read him, therefore; and again, and again; and if then you do not like him, surely you are in some manifest danger, not to understand him." This last word for the guidance of readers of our great poet I should rate above the largest and dullest book that has ever been written on that favorite but supererogatory topic: How to study Shakespeare.

And now our great first laureate in Shakespeare's praise takes about him his singing robes and attires his head with the laurel, his lyre in hand. But the

flowers of his eulogy are ever rooted in the wholesome
soil of judicious criticism. I should like to transcribe
here every word of this splendid poem. " To the memory of my beloved author the Master William Shakespeare and what he hath left us " because I know — to
perpetuate an Irish bull — that only those who have
never really read it can possibly object to reading it
again. But perhaps we had better go on picking out
our seeds and kernels. Jonson opens his poem with
the frank statement that Shakespeare's works are so
superlative in their excellence that " neither man nor
Muse " can overpraise them, and then settles the question of Shakespeare's reception by his contemporaries
with the affirmation " 'tis true and all men's suffrage."
Next he names Chaucer, and Spenser, only to declare
these, " great but disproportioned Muses " as compared with Shakespeare who, contrasted with his
" peers " in the drama of his own time, the critic af-
firms " outshines " them all. Allowing Shakespeare's
" small Latin and less Greek " — which makes his
achievement only the more remarkable in Jonson's
eyes — the eulogist rises to even a higher comparison
and still addressing Shakespeare, calls forth:

> Thund'ring Æschylus,
> Euripides, and Sophocles to us,
> Paccuvius, Accius, him of Cordova dead,
> To life again, to hear thy buskin tread,
> And shake a stage: or, when thy socks were on,
> Leave thee alone, for the comparison
> Of all, that insolent Greece or haughty Rome
> Sent forth, or since did from their ashes come.

And the eloquent passage concludes with the memorable line which is Shakespeare's all-sufficient eulogy and epitaph:

> He was not of an age, but for all time!

Do you know of any subsequent appreciation which equals this in its certainty, its splendor and its truth? With a knowledge of this contemporary estimate of the master poet by the master critic of his own time can we go on ignorantly declaring that the greatness of Shakespeare was questionable in his own age and that he has only come into his own with the growth of modern taste and discernment? Can we continue to believe that, forgotten by his own people, he was only discovered by some German professor or other a century or so ago by reason of congenital German kinship with Shakespeare's genius?

And now we come upon the tribute to the realism — I should rather call it the faithful reality — of Shakespeare's art.

> All the Muses still were in their prime,
> When like Apollo he came forth to warm
> Our ears, or like a Mercury to charm!
> Nature herself was proud of his designs,
> And joy'd to wear the dressing of his lines!
> Which were so richly spun, and woven so fit,
> As, since, she will vouchsafe no other wit.
> The merry Greek, tart Aristophanes,
> Neat Terence, witty Plautus, now not please;
> But antiquated, and deserted lie
> As they were not of Nature's family.

Then follow these remarkable words from the critic of classical leanings who had found Shakespeare " wanting in art."

> Yet must I not give Nature all: thy art,
> My gentle Shakespeare, must enjoy a part.
> For though the poet's matter, nature be,
> His art doth give the fashion. And, that he,
> Who casts to write a living line, must sweat,
> (Such as thine are) and strike the second heat
> Upon the Muses' anvil: turn the same,
> (And himself with it) that he thinks to frame;
> Or for the laurel, he may gain a scorn,
> For a good poet's made, as well as born.
> And such wert thou. Look how the father's face
> Lives in his issue, even so, the race
> Of Shakespeare's mind, and manners brightly shines
> In his well torned, and true-filed lines:
> In each of which, he seems to shake a lance,
> As brandish't at the eyes of ignorance.

Were my discourse of the fronds and tendrils of the jungle of criticism with which we began, how many are the books — some of them very recent — which have sprung out of this discerning recognition of Shakespeare as a metrist, a dramatist, a poet, a man of art, consummate and unmatchable? And the poem concludes with this burst of eloquence in which I doubt not that you will discern sundry familiar quotations:

> Sweet swan of Avon! what a sight it were
> To see thee in our waters yet appear,
> And make those flights upon the banks of Thames,
> That so did take Eliza, and our James!

45

But stay, I see thee in the hemisphere
Advanc'd, and made a constellation there!
Shine forth, thou star of poets, and with rage,
Or influence, chide, or cheer the drooping stage;
Which, since thy flight from hence, hath mourn'd like night,
And despairs day, but for thy volume's light.

But, you may ask, was there, then, no other comment and criticism of Shakespeare in his day? Yes, a plenty of comment, applause, appreciation, as that interesting work *The Shakespeare Allusion Book* abundantly discloses — but not criticism, unless we may so designate adjectives like "mellifluous," "honey-tongued" or an occasional statement that he was possessed of a "facetious grace in writing" or was "excellent in the quality he professes" (that is acting), and "in both kinds of drama for the stage." [6] There is one exception to this general dearth, the exhorting bookseller's preface to the quarto of *Troilus and Cressida*, 1609, which extols the "brain that never undertook anything comical vainly" and in which this remarkable prophecy is hazarded, the poet being yet alive: "Believe this, that when he is gone, and his comedies are out of sale, you will scramble for them and set up a new English inquisition," which I take it to mean signifies a house-to-house search for these valuable contemporary quartos: assuredly here is the very spirit of divination.

Here, for what I have set forth, is then my claim for Jonson as the pod containing the seeds out of which practically all that has proved truly fruitful in our

[6] Ed. Gollancz, 1909, 2 vols. *passim.*

aesthetic criticism and estimate of Shakespeare has actually grown. Jonson is England's first judicial critic. The bulk of his running comment on his time has been, as we have seen, unhappily lost, although we hear again and again echoes of a *bon mot,* an anecdote and have even the delightful code of laws of Jonson's own making in Latin and English which governed those glorious *noctes ambrosianae* in the Apollo room of the Devil Tavern, as earlier at the Mermaid. Of Jonson's literary creed much exists in print, theory and practice alike, in his works. As to his opinions about Shakespeare, we have but little, but what we have is precious and unmistakable, much of it, in its characteristic mixture of learning, which reined Jonson in, and the honest appreciation of a warm heart, which spurred him on. It was the latter which achieved the victory, affirmed by the critic's good sense in his mature verdict, the splendid poem which we have just discussed and which Jonson carefully signed. Importance is to be attached to Jonson's opinions, be it repeated, because he was the critical dictator of his age with scarcely a voice to dissent; and because, above all, Jonson was a competent witness of his time from his intelligence, his honesty and his unparalleled opportunities. Still again an especial value inheres in Jonson's criticism of Shakespeare because so much in Jonson was antithetical to Shakespeare's romantic temper and to the magnificent spendthrift lavishness of his art.

Lastly, what is the Shakespeare that Jonson discloses to us? A ready writer, a lover, a happy portrayer and knower of nature in a large sense of that abused word, which I beseech you to believe must contain human nature as well as horticulture; an artist, in the processes of his technique, a dramatist and poet unparalleled in his own age and country and even among Ben Jonson's own best beloved ancients; a great writer appreciated absolutely and to the full and for his best by his own age; one whose plays have had their triumphant trial and stand above all like achievement "by all men's suffrage." And finally a man to whom preëminently attached the adjective " gentle " which, in the old tongue, be it remembered, signified one endowed with the sum total of those qualities of mind and heart which constitute the veritable gentleman.

Why not take this honest old critic's advice as to our master poet and " read him, therefore, and again and again? " And if you are appalled by the critics and the contradictory things that they persist in telling us, why not seek refuge in the simplicity, the good sense and the sound opinion of rare Ben Jonson?

IV

THE SHAKESPEARE CANON

THERE is an old monograph extant by a logical and exhaustive professor which, listing every error, eccentricity and perversity of scholarship on the topic of Shakespearean authorship, makes out a list of sixty plays, in whole or in part at least, the product of his pen.[1] The cue in that old, discredited Victorian time was to lose no ascertainable scrap which by any possibility may have been his. Under this " canon " the ascriptions of piratical publishers eager to turn a penny, the suggestions of scholars inflating a reputation, or of forgers attempting a sensation, all were accepted. Several plays were even attracted into the Shakespearean category because " who else was there who could possibly have written them? "

But the spirit of the " Shakespeare Canon " has now changed. We have progressed in the arithmetic of the criticism of our great poet from addition to subtraction; and the game now is to question everything and by tests of style, meter and parallel, tests aesthetic and especially psychological, to deprive Shakespeare of every passage in which he is not veritably at his best

[1] R. Sachs, " Die Shakespeare zugeschreibenen zweifelhaften Stücke " *Shakespeare Jahrbuch*, xxvii, 135.

— or is it, perhaps, at our best? What business has
the greatest of our dramatists ever to have written below himself? When he puns execrably, or goes to
pieces according to our enlightened twentieth-century
opinions, when he falls below our standards of taste,
or is brutal or banal — " I don't believe he wrote that
passage " settles the whole matter. And if you are
learned or want to seem learned, it adds immensely to
the effect to add: " That elemental psychology is Marlowe's, this passage discloses the phraseology and vocabulary of Greene, that piece of banality is in the
manner of Peele." And in such a juncture, never forget to mention the percentage of double endings.

However, to be fair, Mr. Robertson has written a
very striking book,[2] in which, pursuing the method of
several previous books of his, he seeks to determine the
limitations of Shakespeare's authorship, this time in
Henry V, Julius Caesar and *Richard III.* Aside from
a nice weighing of matters of verse, style, vocabulary,
taste, construction and dramatic power, much is made
of parallels, likenesses and similarities in idea and expression to plays and passages by Shakespeare's fellow dramatists. *Richard III* has long been thought
Marlovian in conception and in style. Some have
considered it not unnatural that a young aspirant
for dramatic success might have knowingly endeavored to write like his most successful competitor.
But Mr. Robertson will have none of this. The play
to him is Marlowe's. Indeed, by his assiduous processes, Mr. Robertson has deprived Shakespeare not

[2] *The Shakespeare Canon,* by J. M. Robertson, 1922.

only of *Richard* but of the greater part of *Henry V*, including the fine choruses which we would fain have kept; and he has left Shakespeare in *Julius Caesar* not even Antony's famous speech over the body of Caesar. *Henry,* it seems, was " rough hewn " by Marlowe, expanded by Greene, and perhaps Peele, and contains besides " Chapmanesque speeches " and suspicions of Jonson. Shakespeare may possibly have touched it up; but, as a whole, he was incapable of anything so " bad." As to Antony's famous speech, " the intolerable metaphor " as to the wounds in Caesar's body, which are likened to " dumb mouths " which " do ope their ruby lips," settles the matter, especially because this dreadful figure occurs in a certain obscure murder play. Mr. Robertson's Shakespeare never uses a figure previously employed by anyone else; Mr. Robertson's Shakespeare never wrote tastelessly or beneath the standard fastidiously set for him by Mr. Robertson.

The mere scholar stands aghast at the virtuosity of this surprising critic. He can spot you a line of Marlowe, Jonson, Chapman, Heywood, whom you will, anywhere and in anybody's alleged writing. Greene cannot elude him, nor Lyly escape. Poor Kit Marlowe, with his scarce seven years of authorship, is worked nearly to death. He could have had little time for atheism. A similarity in places, the use of an unusual word, a bit of boastful rhetoric and especially a percentage of something or other connected with meter, and the trick is turned. According to the " results " of this kind of criticism, the Elizabethan dramatists collaborated universally and promiscuously, meddling and intermeddling with each other's work, irrespective of time, place, ownership or rivalry. Neither friendship nor enmity deterred them, and they borrowed, stole, and juggled each with the writings of each other with the abandon of a bevy of idiots playing logomachy. The marvel is that any of their productions are readable at all.

Indubitably the age of Shakespeare was much given to collaboration and plays were habitually rewritten, altered and revised, frequently by hands other than the original author's. Tarleton's old *Henry V* may have been succeeded by other versions of the " history " before Shakespeare took up the theme, and it is not " impossible " — but Mr. Robertson does not prove it — that another play may have intervened. But the point is not here, but in an essential misconception as to Shakespeare. Our foremost poet and dramatist is a very unequal author. In him indeed is " the front of Jove "; but he too was young once and inexperienced, and he was often hurried and careless; and, dare we say it, perhaps even indolent at times as to doing his best. The late Dr. Horace Howard Furness, when he read *Cymbeline,* used to rise, when he came to the banalities of the dreams and visions of Posthumus towards the end, with the observation: " At this point Shakespeare lost all interest in his subject and naturally so do we." Inequality, imitation of the gait and manner of other men, indifference as to trifles, want of taste, inconsistency, all of these things are true of Shakespeare in places. But we need not for these reasons "relieve" him of the creation of an ignoble Caesar and a monstrous Richard — both of which Mr. Robertson puts on his packhorse Marlowe — nor of an inconsistent Portia, whom he fathers on Ben Jonson, or is it Chapman?

Perhaps we might put aside this example of a skeptic, devoid of faith in anything except his own surprising powers of discernment. But this species of "revision" of our accepted opinions as to Shakespeare and his works has become a striking feature of much of even our authoritative contemporary scholarship. On the latest volume of *The New [Cambridge] Shakespeare, The Merchant of Venice,* a recent reviewer comments pertinently as follows:

> Here is the perfect example of Shakespeare at his work as the popular Elizabethan entertainer. In it personal and impersonal are inextricably blended. Can the modern critic stomach it? The new Cambridge editors apparently cannot. At one end of the new volume is Sir Arthur Quiller-Couch busy boring holes in it as a work of art; at the other, is the implacable geologist, Dr. Dover Wilson, detecting stratum after stratum in the upheaved mountain, but with an eye that grows yearly keener for the primeval non-Shakespearean basalt. The strategy of the two editors is strictly according to Moltke: *getrennt marchieren, vereint schlagen.* The scenes and portions of scenes they reject as non-Shakespearean would be almost enough to set up a new Elizabethan playwright in business.[3]

That the editing of Shakespeare is not a task for the uninitiate, the innumerable "commentaries" of those who have rushed in where scholars fear to tread afford a more than sufficient example. Shakespeare

---

[3] *London Times Literary Supplement,* June 17, 1926, p. 410.

is heady wine, and even the strong have been exhilarated by him to unwonted temerity or bewildered into guesswork and uncertainty. As to his workmanship for the playhouse, Shakespeare rose like the sun obscured in the vapors of collaboration; and he set, too, with similar clouds dimming his brightness. Precisely how much of the earlier plays may be the residue of work by Marlowe, Greene, Peele, or even lesser men, we cannot ever hope to " know," unless endowed with a sixth sense for the detection of stylistic and metrical niceties, such as Mr. Robertson claims for himself; a sense, it is not to be denied, often cleverly enough invoked, if not always quite convincingly, for Shakespeare as well as for the work of others. In like manner we recognize the assiduity of those who have endeavored to tell us precisely the terms and limitations of the temporary partnership in authorship, which appears to have been Shakespeare's towards the end of his life, with Fletcher, and perhaps Massinger as well.[4] And again and again we find ourselves " convinced " it may be by the immediate argument, but slipping back into a stubborn misbelief when, the pleadings withdrawn, we ponder the case at ease, weighed in the scales of average credibility. Is it unfair to surmise that contemporary scholarship, especially in Shakespeare, is somewhat more apt to assume the argumentativeness of the advocate than to rest serene in the dispassionateness of the judge?

Let us return for the nonce to collaboration in playwriting, a matter of crucial importance if we are bent

[4] E. H. C. Oliphant, *The Plays of Beaumont and Fletcher*, 1927.

to fix once and for all the precise limitation of Shakespeare's hand in every scrap of his work. A pertinent monograph a few years ago distinguished several kinds of collaboration among Elizabethan dramatists.[5] There was the crude method of meting out the play act by act, sometimes to as many writers as there were acts, more commonly to two or three authors. These appear at times to have worked more or less separately and in their joinings the joints are often visible. This was no unusual method among the henchmen of Philip Henslowe, theatrical promoter and moneyed man who controlled so much of the popular dramatic output of Shakespeare's rivals. But, strange as may appear, it seems likewise to have been the practice at times among the young gentlemen of the Inns of Court in their efforts to entertain their friends and their queen. A more rational collaboration was that in which each of two coadjutors took a plot. Such appears to have been the method of Middleton and Rowley; and an even more vital association was conceivably that of Beaumont and Fletcher, in which each wrote the scene for which his talents best fitted him and the completed product must have been the result of a coöperation alike of plan and of criticism.

But there was quite another kind of joint authorship. Even in Shakespeare's alleged participancy with Fletcher in say *Henry VIII*, to what extent was this not the work of coequals, but a case of the retouching of an older play by one or other of the alleged authors?

[5] E. N. S. Thompson, "Elizabethan Collaboration," *Englische Studien*, xi, 30.

And who did the retouching? Working, as the Elizabethans habitually did, with previous dramatic material their preferred quarry, revision, rewriting, manipulation, adaptation was as much the vogue of the playmakers as was the altering of costumes a function of the custodians of the wardrobe. Wherefore a justification for the existence of the " implacable geologist . . . detecting stratum after stratum in the upheaved mountain with an eye that grows yearly keener for the primeval non-Shakespearean basalt." Wherefore, too, *Measure for Measure,* for example, " offers problems to the bibliographical detective of quite exceptional interest and complexity "; and we learn, as a result of his labors — in this case those of Dr. Dover Wilson — that the text of this play has been abridged; secondly that it has also elsewhere been expanded; and that these two revisions were not simultaneous, but were " undertaken at some years' interval and possibly by different dramatists." Further even than this, " it is conceivable," we are told, " that there may have been later revisions still, before the text reached the hands of the printer." Indeed, Dr. Wilson finds " at least a presumption that the folio text of *Measure for Measure* contains additions by a post-Shakespeare reviser," and concludes:

" If we imagine that the abridgment of 1604 was made from the existing players' parts and not on Shakespeare's MS, that this original unabridged MS. was afterwards lost, and that the prose adapter, therefore, constructed his text from the players' parts of 1604, hastily transcribing them and filling out the play with additions of his own, we are making a not unreasonable guess as to the origin of the actual copy used for the printing of *Measure for Measure* as we have it." [6]

"A not unreasonable guess!" But is it no more than this that this busy formidable scholarship can do for us? And is this same puzzling play, with all the differences of opinion as to its personages and their conduct, really so disastrous a hodge-podge, when all is said? Moreover, if it is, could it produce the powerful effect which follows alike the reading or the seeing of it? It is one of the miracles of Shakespeare that with all this searching into his defects, with all this evidence as to the utter hopelessness of these helter-skelter texts of his, corrupt, interpolated, carelessly abridged or stupidly expanded, we still contrive to read them and to get a pleasure out of them, corruptions and all, which the carefully groomed productions of later ages cannot afford us. As of two evils, so of two incredibilities, — prefer the less. Those who are shaping for us anew the Shakespeare Canon demand of us a deeper faith in the results of their devastating inquisitions than genius has ever invoked of reader or auditor to excuse the inconsistencies of his resources or the inadequacy of his powers. It is difficult, in a word, to believe results so admirable the product of methods so chaotic — and this even when we must qualify our admiration, as we must for disquieting *Measure for Measure*, unsatisfying *All's Well*, and bitter, disenchanting *Troilus and Cressida*.

Much more might be said of other means employed to shape anew the canon of the Shakespearean plays.

[6] Cambridge Shakespeare, *Measure for Measure*, 1922, p. 113.

Bibliography has been powerfully invoked, indubitably to set us straight in much that appertains to the printed word. Especially have the relations of the texts of the quartos and the folios been revised in the scholarly work of Pollard, Greg, and others. And in one conspicuous example at least the canon has extended Shakespeare's range of authorship by the suggestion, not idly to be set aside despite the criticism of Schücking or Tannenbaum, that in one of the scenes of the manuscript play, *Sir Thomas More*, we have a piece of Shakespeare's authorship written by his own hand.[7] In the wider reaches of the subject the question "what is the nature of the errors which given peculiarities in the handwriting of the manuscript are likely to beget in the printed copy" indicates, with other kindred queries, new possibilities for " the bibliographical detective," to say no more. The ingenuity of our age has invented many new tools. But sharp tools are useful only in trained and intelligent hands; and the sharpest are the most readily put to the most dangerous misuse. It is asking perhaps too much of this generation of ours that it come to a full realization of the truth as to two of its obsessions: that the methods of our triumphant science are not applicable with their " certainties of result " to everything under the sun; and secondly, that there are many questions — the precise limitation of Shakespeare's authorship among them — against which we can never hope to write the definitive Q. E. D.

---

[7] See *Review of English Studies*, Jan. 1925; and *Studies in Philology*, 1925, xxii, 133.

V

BEN JONSON AND THE CLASSICAL SCHOOL

WITHOUT here threshing out again an old-time harvest which has been beaten to the last grain, it may none the less be not impertinently premised that the words, classical and romantic, those overworked counters in the small change of criticism, have been taken by the present writer, both here and elsewhere, to designate tendencies rather than opposed methods in art; and that the former, together with much else, seems to him to lean to the realization of artistic things along the line of tradition and correctness according to some previous standard, while the latter substitutes an effort after freedom from restraint and a realization of beauty and significance in things new, strange or at least out of the ordinary. A further canon of the present writer's acceptance is his conviction that literature has always partaken of both the tendency which conserves and the tendency which seeks after the novel and the strange; and that a literary age may be called classic or romantic, not in the absence of either, but in the domination of one tendency over the other at a given time. Indeed we may surmise that in the ebb and flow of these elements consists the very life of art, and that in an approximate triumph of either over the other we can have either the death of stagnation or the annihilation of chaos. It is at least as old as Stendhal that every "classic" had once the novelty of the "romantic" in it. And even romantic excess, grown common, may become distasteful from the loss of that which once made it romantic. The romantic temper, in a word, studies the past, the classic neglects it. The romantic temper is empirical. In its successful experiments it lays the foundations for classics to come. It is the failures and excesses of romanticism that bring us trooping back to the classics to find with Matthew Arnold "The only sure guidance, the only solid footing among the ancients." [1]

With these bases of dogmatism to stand on, we may note that the history of English literature since the Renaissance exhibits three periods of unusual interest in the models of the past, three notable returns to the classics as they were understood in each age. An important name is identified with each: Sir Philip Sidney, whose classicism was concerned with externals, and soon overwhelmed with the flood of romanticism on which he was himself "the first fair freight;" Ben Jonson, whose classicism came alike by nature and by study; and Pope, who long after stands for the culmination of a movement which, losing its aims and substituting too often mere form for living principle, is none the less worthy of a greater respect and consid-

[1] See the earlier formulation of these ideas on the basis of Pater's well known *Appreciations* in the first draught of this paper, *Publications of the Modern Language Association*, 1898, xiii.

eration than has been accorded it at the hands of some of the critics.

That minor contemporaries of Sidney like Ascham, Webbe, and Gabriel Harvey should look to classic example for the salvation of English letters is little to be wondered. Their education demanded it, and contemporary literature offered nothing. Save Chaucer, there was not an English poet that a scholar dared to name with the mighty dead of " insolent Greece or haughty Rome "; and Chaucer was antiquated to the Elizabethan, who might love to archaize in the pastoral lingo of Hobbinol and Cuddy, but who was likely to leave unread what he could not readily shape into conformity with his own time and situation. The classicism of Sidney is that of his age, and shows itself mainly in two characteristics: the reaffirmation of ancient aesthetic theory and in metrical experiments in English verse modelled on classical prosody. In the former Sidney was the companion of Gascoigne, King James, Webbe, and the author of *The Art of English Poesy;* [2] in the latter, of Harvey, Stanihurst, Fraunce, and Spenser himself. If Sidney's sapphics and asclepiads stand as a warning to the temerity of venturesome youth, it must be remembered that our late Victorian contemporaries did not cease from theorizing upon such meters nor indeed from imitating them. Such turning to the classics as Sidney's or Spenser's is purely empirical and due less to any deep-seated conviction on the subject than to a contempla-

[2] *Review of English Studies,* i, 300, 1925, where this book is assigned to the authorship of John Lord Lumley.

tion of the dead level of contemporary literary achievement. Sidney's *Defense of Poesy* was directly called forth by Gosson's attack on poetry in his *School of Abuse,* and Sidney's own practice of classical meters went hand in hand with experiments in the Italian sonnet, the canzone and the sestine, many specimens of which are to be found in *Astrophel and Stella,* and in the *Arcadia.* And yet, it would be difficult to find a work farther removed from classical ideals than the famous *Arcadia* itself, the story of which vies with the *Faery Queen* in rambling involution and elaborated episode, the style of which is ornate and florid, though often very beautiful, the essence of which, in a word, is novelty, the touchstone of romantic art.

Vastly in contrast with this superficial imitation of classical verse is the classicism of Ben Jonson, a classicism grounded in his character as a man and a scholar. Between Sidney, dead in the year 1586, and Jonson, beginning his career but a year or two short of the new century, a great literature had sprung up, which, to the end of the reign of Elizabeth and without the domain of the drama, was dominated by the overwhelming influence of Spenser. It would be difficult to find a contrast more marked than that which exists between Spenser and Jonson. As the qualities of these two poets in their contrasts are at the very root of our subject, they must be considered in some detail.

What may be called the manner of Spenser — *i.e.,* Spenser's way of imitating and interpreting nature artistically by means of poetic expression — may be summarized as consisting of a sensuous love of beauty, involving a power of elaborated pictorial representation, a use of classical imagery for decorative effect, a fondness for melody of sound, a flowing sweetness, naturalness and continuousness of diction, amounting to diffuseness at times, the diffuseness of a fragrant, beautiful, flowering vine. We may say of the poets that employ this manner that they are worshipers of beauty rather than students of beauty's laws; ornate in their expression of the type, dwelling on detail in thought and image lovingly elaborated and sweetly prolonged. To such artists it is no matter if a play have five acts or twenty-five, if an epic ever come to an end, or if consistency of parts exist. Rapt in the joy of gentle onward motion, in the elevation of pure, poetic thought, even the subject seems to be of small import, if it but furnish the channel in which the bright limpid liquid continues musically to flow. Drayton, who, besides pastorals after the manner of his master, Spenserized the enormous *Polyolbion;* the allegorical Fletchers, Giles and Phineas; George Wither and William Browne in their beautiful later pastorals; Milton himself in his earliest poetry, though somewhat restrained by a chaster taste than was Spenser's and by a spirit in closer touch with the classics: these are some of the followers and imitators of Spenser.

If now we turn to the poetry of Ben Jonson, more especially to his non-dramatic verse, the first thing we note is a sense of form, not merely in detail and transition, like the " links . . . bright and even " of *The Faery Queen,* but a sense of the entire poem in its relation to its parts. This sense involves brevity and condensity of expression, a feeling on the part of the poet that the effect may be spoiled by a word too much — a feeling which no true Spenserian ever knew. It is thus that Jonson deftly turns an epitaph:

> Wouldst thou hear what man can say
> In a little? Reader, stay:
> Underneath this stone doth lie
> As much beauty as could die;
> Which in life did harbor give
> To more virtue than doth live.
> If at all she had a fault,
> Leave it buried in this vault.
> One name was Elizabeth,
> Th'other, let it sleep with death:
> Fitter where it died to tell,
> Than that it lived at all. Farewell.

About such poetry as this there is a sense of finish rather than of elaboration. It is less continuous than complete; more concentrated, less diffuse, chaste rather than florid, controlled, and yet not always less spontaneous, reserved, and yet not always less natural. There are other things in the Jonsonian manner. It retained classical allusion less for the sake of embellishment than as an atmosphere — to borrow a term from the nomenclature of art. Its drafts upon ancient mythology become allusive, and the effects produced by Horace, Catullus or Anacreon are essayed in reproduction under English conditions. Not less eager in the pursuit of beauty than the Spenserian, the manner of Jonson seeks to realize her perfections by means of constructive excellence, not by entranced passion. It concerns itself with choiceness of diction, selectiveness in style, with the repression of wandering ideas and loosely conceived figures, in a word, the manner of Jonson involves classicality. Sidney's return to the ancients has been called *empirical;* the classicism of Jonson may be termed *assimilative.*

It is a commonplace of the history of literature that Jonson literally dominated the age in which he lived. But it is not so generally understood just why this was true in the face of the unexampled popularity of Shakespeare's plays and the frequent failure of Jonson's own, and with the existence of strong poetical counter-influences which seemed more typical of the spirit of the time than Jonson's own. It is notable that it is the egotists, like Byron and Rousseau, who impress themselves upon their own times; they are, in Ben Jonson's well known words, " of an age "; those who have mastered themselves and risen, as did Shakespeare, above their own environment while still sharing it, move in larger circles, and influence the world " for all time." Shakespeare was not literary, Jonson was abundantly so. Despite Shakespeare's popular success, Jonson had with him the weight of the court and the learned. Thus it came about that Shakespeare enjoyed the greatest pecuniary return derived from literature, directly or indirectly, until the days of Sir Walter Scott; whilst Jonson, dependent on patronage, often almost in want, achieved a reputation and an influence in literature altogether unsurpassed up to his time. There was only one poet who shared even in part this literary supremacy of Jonson, and that poet was Donne. To

Donne, especially to the concettist in him, must be granted the credit — if credit it be — of delaying for more than a generation the natural revulsion of English literature back to classicism and restraint. This is not the place in which to discuss the interesting relations of Jonson and Donne. Except for a certain rhetorical and dialectical address, which might be referred to a study of the ancients, the poetry of Donne is marked by its disregard of conventions, by its extraordinary originality of thought and expression, by that rare quality of poetic insight that justifies Jonson's enthusiastic claim that " John Donne [was] the first poet in the world in some things." Not less significant on the other hand are Jonson's contrasted remarks to Drummond on the same topic: " That Donne's ' Anniversary ' [in which true womanhood is idealized if not deified] was profane and full of blasphemies," and " that Donne, for not keeping of accent, deserved hanging." [3] The classicist has always regarded the romanticist thus, nor have the retorts been more courteous, as witness the well known lines of Keats' " Sleep and Poetry " in which the age of classicism is summarily dismissed as " a schism nurtured by foppery and barbarism."

Thus we find Spenser and Jonson standing as exponents respectively of the expansive or romantic movement and the repressive or classical spirit. In a different line of distinction Donne is equally in contrast with Spenser, as the intensive, or subjective artist. Both of these latter are romanticists in that each seeks to pro-

[3] *Conversations*, Shakespeare Society, 1842, 8 and 3.

duce the effect demanded of art by means of an appeal to the sense of novelty; but Spenser's romanticism is that of selection, which chooses from the outer world the fitting and the pleasing, and constructs it into a permanent artistic joy. Donne's is the romanticism of insight, which, looking inward, descries the subtle relations of things and transmutes them into poetry with a sudden and unexpected flood of light. Between Jonson and Donne there is the kinship of intellectuality; between Spenser and Donne the kinship of romanticism; between Spenser and Jonson the kinship of the poet's joy in beauty. Spenser is the most objective and therefore allegorical and mystical; Donne is the most subjective and the most spiritual; Jonson, the most artistic and therefore the most logical.

But not only did Jonson dominate his age and stand for the classical ideal in the midst of current Spenserianism, concettist and other popular modes, it was this position of Jonson, defended as it was in theory as well as exemplified in his work, that directed the course which English literature was to take for a century and a half after his death. There are few subjects in the history of literature attended with greater difficulty than the attempt to explain how the lapse of a century in time should have transformed the literature of England from the traits which characterized it in the reign of Queen Elizabeth to those which came to prevail under the rule of Queen Anne. The salient characteristics of the two ages are much too well known to call for repetition here. Few readers, moreover, are unfamiliar with the more usual theories on this subject: how one critic believes that Edmund Waller invented the new poetry by a spontaneous exercise of his own cleverness; how another demands that this responsibility be fixed upon George Sandys.[4] How some think that "classicism" was an importation from France, which came into England in the luggage of the fascinating Frenchwoman, who afterwards became the Duchess of Portsmouth; and how still others suppose that the whole thing was really in the air, to be caught by infection by anyone who did not draw apart and live out of the literary miasma as did Milton. It may not be unnecessary to add that some of these theorists place the beginning and end of "classicism" in the definite and peculiar construction of a certain species of English decasyllabic verse; and that even when they escape this, the "heroic" or "Popean couplet" has always usurped an undue share of consideration.

The conservative reaction which triumphed with the Restoration has been so "hardly entreated" and so bitterly scorned that there is much temptation to attempt a justification. Imaginative literature did lose in the change, and enormously; but if the imagination, and with it the power that produces poetry, became for a time all but extinct, the understanding, or power which arranges, correlates, expounds and explains, went through a course of development which has brought with it in the end nothing but gain to the literature considered as a whole.

[4] Gosse, *Eighteenth Century Literature*, p. 2. Henry Wood, "Beginnings of the 'Classical' Heroic Couplet in England." *American Journal of Philology*, xi, p. 73.

If the reader will consider the three great names, Ben Jonson, finishing his work about 1635, Dryden, at the height of his fame fifty years later, and Pope, with nearly ten years of literary activity before him a century after Jonson's death, he will notice certain marked differences in a general resemblance in the range, subject-matter and diction of the works of these three. The plays of Jonson, despite the restrictive character of his genius, exemplify nearly the whole spacious field of Elizabethan drama, with two added successes, the invention of the comedy of humors and the development of the masque, which are Jonson's own. Jonson is the first poet who gave to occasional verse that variety of subject, that power and finish, which made it, for nearly two centuries, the most important form of poetical expression. The works of Jonson are pervaded with satire, criticism and translation, though all appear less in set form than as applied to original work. Finally Jonson's lyrics maintain the diversity, beauty and originality which distinguishes this species of poetry in his favored age.

If we turn now to Dryden, we find still a wide range in subject, although limitations are discoverable in the character of his dramas and of his lyrics. If we except his operas and those pseudo-dramatic aberrations in which he adapted the work of Shakespeare and Milton, Dryden writes only two kinds of plays, the heroic drama and the comedy of manners; whilst his lyrics, excepting the two odes for Saint Cecelia's Day and some perfunctory religious poems, are wholly amatory in the narrow and vitiated sense in which that term was employed in the time of Charles II. The strongest element of Dryden's work is occasional verse; and he makes a new departure, showing the tendency of the time, in the development of what may be called occasional prose: the preface and dedicatory epistle. Satire takes form in the translation of Juvenal and in the author's own brilliant original satires, translation becomes Dryden's most lucrative literary employment, and criticism is the very element in which he lives. Lastly, we turn to Pope. Here are no plays and very few lyrics, scarcely one which is not an applied poem. Occasional verse, satire, criticism, and translation have usurped the whole field. There was no need that Pope should write his criticism in prose, as did Dryden; for verse had become in his hands essentially the medium for the expression of that species of thought which we now habitually associate with the prose form. Indeed the verse of Pope was more happily fitted for the expression of the thought of Pope, than any prose that could possibly have been devised; for Pope's demand was for a medium in which rhetorical brilliancy and telling antithesis was a treasure to be coveted above precision of thought.

It has often been affirmed that England's is the greater poetry, while France possesses the superior prose; and in the confusion or distinction of the two species of literature this difference has been explained. Poetry must be governed by the imagination, it must not only see and imitate, it must transform what it sees, converting the actual into the terms of the ideal:

if it does much beside, it is less poetry. On the other hand, prose is a matter of the understanding, to call in as helps whatever other faculty you will, but to be ruled and governed by the intelligence alone, to the end that the object may be realized as it actually *is*. With this distinction before us, when passion, real or simulated, when imagination, genuine or forced, takes the reins from the understanding, the product may become poetry, or enthusiasm, or rhapsody; it certainly ceases to be prose, good, bad or indifferent. So, likewise, when the understanding supplants imagination, we have also a product, which, whatever its form or the wealth of rhetoric bestowed upon it, is alien to poetry. This is to be interpreted no criticism of the many English literary products, which have the power to run as well as to fly; we could not spare one of the great pages of the prose rhapsodists; and yet it may well be doubted if, on the whole, the French have not been somewhat the gainers from the care with which they have customarily, at least until lately, kept their prose and their poetry sundered.

Up to this point it has been our endeavor to establish the simultaneous existence of the restrictive as well as the romantic element in our literature as early as the reign of Elizabeth, to show the relation of the one to the other in the stretch of years that elapsed from her reign to that of Queen Anne, and to exemplify the relation of Jonson (who is claimed to be the exponent of the classical spirit) to his immediate contemporaries and to his two most typical successors. Let us now examine some of the reasons which may be urged for placing Jonson in so prominent a position.

In Ben Jonson we have the earliest example of the interesting series of English literary men who have had definite theories about literature. Dryden, Pope, and Wordsworth were such, each potent in moulding the taste of his own age, and, with it, the course which literature was to take in times to come. It is notorious that the attitude of Jonson towards the prevalent literary taste of his age was far from conciliatory. He despised the popular judgment with an arrogance unparalleled in the annals of literature, although he constantly professed himself solicitous of the favorable opinion of the judicious. Jonson was a great moralist in his way, and " of all styles he loved most to be named honest "; but he was likewise an artist, and many of his current criticisms of his contemporaries: his strictures on Shakespeare for his anachronisms, on Sidney for making all the characters of the *Arcadia* speak like gentlemen and gentlewomen, his objection to the obscurity and irregular versification of Donne, are referable to an outraged aesthetic sense.[5] This position was altogether conscious, the position of the professional man who has a theory to oppose to the amateurishness and eclecticism abundantly exemplified in contemporary work; and Jonson must have felt toward the glittering, multiform literature of Elizabeth much what Matthew Arnold suffered " amid the bewildering confusion of our times " and might well have exclaimed with him, " I seemed to myself to find the

[5] *Conversations*, 37, 16, 2 and 3.

only sure guidance, the only solid footing, among the ancients. They, at any rate, knew what they wanted in art, and we do not. It is this uncertainty which is disheartening." [6]

The theories which Ben Jonson held about literature were from the first those of the classicist. He believed in the criticism of Horace and in the rhetoric of Quintilian; in the sanction of classical usage for history, oratory, and poetry.[7] He believed that English drama should follow the example of the *vetus comoedia*,[8] and that an English ode should be modelled faithfully on the structural niceties of Pindar. Despite all this, Jonson's theories about literature were not only, in the main, reasonable and consistent, they were often surprisingly liberal. Thus he could laugh, as he did, in a well known passage of the prologue to *Every Man in His Humor*, at the absurdities of contemporary stage realism which,

> with three rusty swords,
> And help of some few foot-and-half-foot words,
> Fight over York and Lancaster's long jars;
> And in the tiring-house bring wounds to scars;

and yet declare, as to that fetish of the supine classicist, the three unities, that "we [English playwrights] should enjoy the same licence or free power to illustrate and heighten our invention as they [the an-

---

[6] Preface to *Poems*, ed. 1854.

[7] See the many passages of the *Discoveries* which are no more than translations of the *Institutes*, and the weight given to the theories of Horace in the same book.

[8] Prologue to *Every Man out of his Humor*.

73

cients] did; and not be tied to those strict and regular forms which the niceness of a few, who are nothing but form, would thrust upon us." He could affirm that " Spenser's stanzas pleased him not, nor his matter "; and yet tell Drummond that "for a heroic poem there was no such ground as King Arthur's fiction " (i.e. the legends concerning King Arthur). He censured the pastoralists for their unreality, and yet he had by heart passages of the *Shepherds' Calendar* and showed how to write a true pastoral drama in the *Sad Shepherd;* he mocked the sonneteers,[9] especially Daniel, in his satirical plays, for their sugared sweetness and frivolity, but wrote himself some of the finest lyrics of his age. The catholicity of Jonson's taste in his sympathy included the philosophy and eloquence of Lord Bacon, the divinity of Hooker, the historical and antiquarian enquiries of Camden and Selden, the classical scholarship of Chapman and the poetry of such diverse men as Spenser, Father Southwell, Donne, Sandys, Herrick, Carew, and his own lesser " sons."

The characteristics of Jonson as the exponent of the conservative spirit in literature in an age conspicuous for its passionate love of novelty are somewhat these: an unusual acquaintance with the literature of Greece and Rome, a holding of " the prose writers and poets of antiquity," to employ the happy phrase of Symonds, " in solution in his spacious memory," and a marvelous ability to pour them " plastically forth

---

[9] On these points, see the *Conversations*, pp. 5, 74, 2, 10, 9, 4 and elsewhere.

into the mould of thought "; [10] a keen appreciation of the principles which lie at the root of classical literature, with an intelligent recognition and a liberal interpretation of those principles in their adaptation to the needs of contemporary English conditions. The rhetorician in Jonson was alike his distinction and his limitation. It was this which gave him an ever-present sense of an inspiring design, whether it was in the construction of a complete play or in the selection and ordering of the words of a single clause. These more general characteristics of the classicist will be recognized at once as Jonson's; but even the specific qualities that mark the coming age of English classicism are his. We have already remarked Jonson's fondness for satire and criticism, and his exceeding use of that species of applied poetry called occasional verse. Restriction in the range of subject is always attended by a corresponding restriction in style and form, and we are prepared to find in Jonson's occasional verse a strong tendency to precise and pointed antithetical diction, and a somewhat conventionalized and restricted metrical form. If we look at Jonson's prose we shall find other " notes " only less marked of the coming classical supremacy, in his slightly Latinized vocabulary and in his occasional preference for abstract over concrete expression.[11]

Besides Jonson's several strictures on cross rimes,

---

[10] " Ben Jonson," *English Worthies*, p. 52.

[11] See such a passage as that beginning: " There is a difference between mooting and pleading, between fencing and fighting, etc. *Discoveries* p. 16; or: " When a virtuous man is raised, it brings gladness to his friends, grief to his enemies, and glory to his posterity." *Ibid.*, 42.

the stanzas of Spenser, the alexandrine of Drayton, English hexameters and sonnets, the very first entry of the *Conversations* tells us of a projected epic with the added information " it is all in couplets for he detesteth all other rimes." A little below Jonson tells of his having written against Campion's and Daniel's well known treatises on versification to prove " couplets to be the bravest sort of verses, especially when they are broken like hexameters," *i.e.*, exhibit a regular caesural pause.[12]

The non-dramatic verse of Jonson was grouped by the author under the headings " Epigrams " and " The Forest," both published in the folio of 1616, and " Underwoods," miscellaneous poems of the collected edition of 1640. Aside from his strictly lyrical verse in which Jonson shared the metrical inventiveness and variety of his age, the decasyllabic rimed couplet is all but his constant measure. For epistles, elegies, and epigrams, some two hundred poems, he seldom uses any other verse, and he employs this verse in translation and sometimes even for lyric purposes. In Jonson's hands the decasyllabic couplet became the habitual measure for occasional verse, and, sanctioned by his usage, remained such for a hundred and fifty years. But not only did Jonson's theory and practice coincide in his overwhelming preference for this particular form of verse, but the decasyllabic couplet as practised by Jonson exemplifies all the characteristics which, in greater emphasis, came in time to distinguish the manner and versification of Waller and Dry-

12 *Ibid.*, 2, 4, and 1.

den. Moreover, the practice of no other poet exemplifies like characteristics to anything approaching the same extent until we pass beyond the accession of Charles I.

Leaving these two propositions for the nonce, it is a commonplace of the history of English verse that the heroic or decasyllabic couplet became, in the hands of Dryden and especially in those of Pope, the all but universal medium of expression for the thoughts of the poets. More, this verse, in these hands, assumed certain very definite characteristics, of which the chief was a tendency to phrase more and more tersely, by couplets, by single lines, even to the splitting of the line into halves to point by structure the antithetical rhetoric which governed the style of the age. To put this in a different way, the heroic couplet, as popularly used after the Restoration, differs in manner from the decasyllabic couplet as that verse was practised by Spenser, Marlowe and other Elizabethans, and that difference consists mainly in the greater fluidity and continuousness of the Elizabethan mode and its freer phrasing and less mannered employment of that pause in the voice called by metrists the caesura.[13] All that we are concerned with here is to note that Jonson, rather than Sandys or Waller (both of whom followed him in point of date), writes a kind of decasyllabic couplet, early in his career and throughout it, which is more in the subsequent manner of Dryden and Pope than in accord with the practices of other

[13] For more specific data by which this result is substantiated, see the earlier form of this paper.

poets in Jonson's own age. And this returns us to our two propositions above, which may then be accepted with the caveat that it is not in the least assumed that the versification of Jonson, Dryden, and Pope is all reducible to a single definition; but it is claimed that the characteristics of the versification of Jonson's couplets are of the type which, developed through Dryden and Waller, led on logically to the culmination of that type in Pope; and that no possible development of the couplet of Sandys and Spenser could have led to a similar result.

More important, however, than the mannerisms of verse — matters which have been rather overstressed — is the parallel which we find between Jonson and his successors in what may be called the classical manner with its crisp diction, its set figures, its parallel constructions, its contrasted clauses, its inversions. Without pursuing this subject into minute detail, the following passages may be well compared.

In 1660 Dryden wrote thus:

> And welcome now, great monarch, to your own,
> Behold th' approaching cliffs of Albion:
> It is no longer motion cheats your view,
> As you meet it, the land approacheth you.
> The land returns, and in the white it wears,
> The marks of patience and sorrow bears.
> But you, whose goodness your descent doth show
> Your heavenly parentage, and earthly too,
> By that same mildness, which your father's crown
> Before did ravish, shall secure your own.[14]

[14] *Astraea Redux*, Dryden, Globe ed·, 14.

In obvious further development of the same manner, Pope writes some seventy-five years later:

> To thee, the world its present homage pays,
> The harvest early, but mature the praise;
> Great friend of liberty! In kings a name
> Above all Greek, above all Roman fame:
> Whose word is truth, as sacred as revered
> As heav'n's own oracles from altars heard.
> Wonder of kings! like whom to mortal eyes
> None e'er has risen, and none e'er shall rise.[15]

Sandys wrote as follows in 1638, the year after the death of Jonson:

> The Muse, who from your influence took her birth,
> First wandered through the many-peopled earth;
> Next sung the change of things, disclosed th' unknown,
> Then to a nobler shape transformed her own;
> Fetched from Engaddi spice, from Jewry balm,
> And bound her brows with Idumaean palm;
> Now old, hath her last voyage made, and brought
> To royal harbor this her sacred fraught:
> Who to her king bequeaths the wealth of kings,
> And dying, her own epicedium sings.[16]

But Jonson had written thus, near the beginning of the reign of James:

> Who would not be thy subject James, t' obey
> A prince that rules by example more than sway?
> Whose manners draw more than thy powers constrain,
> And in this short time of thy happiest reign,

[15] *First Epistle of the Second Book of Horace, To Augustus*, 1737, Pope, Chandos ed., 313.

[16] Dedication of *A Paraphrase upon Job*. Sandys, ed. *Library of Old Authors*, i, lxxix.

Hast purged thy realms, as we have now no cause
Left us for fear, but first our crimes, then laws.
Like aids 'gainst treason who hath found before?
And than in them how could we know God more?
First thou preservèd wert, our Lord to be,
And since, the whole land was preserv'd in thee.[17]

If now we consider rhetorical structure and remember how true it is of the style of Pope that it is built upon antithesis and parallel construction, word against word, clause against clause, verse against verse, paragraph against paragraph, and what is more important, thought against thought, we shall find an interesting result. There is nothing antithetical in the prevailing style of Sandys, either in his translation — except so far as Hebrew parallelism may easily account for it — or in his original verse. On the other hand Jonson knew the value of antithetical construction and used it with intelligence and frequency, though not, as did later writers, almost to the exclusion of other rhetorical devices. The quotation from Jonson exemplifies antithetical construction in all its subtlety. The *prince* and his *subject* are contrasted; the *prince rules*, the *subject obeys*. The prince rules by *example* more than by *sway;* his *manners draw* more than his *powers constrain.* The subject fears his own *crimes* more than the prince's *laws;* and in the end the prince is preserved to be king, and his subjects are preserved in him; which last antithesis involves " conceit " as it often continued to do in Dryden as

[17] *To King James*, ed. Gifford viii., 162.

80

witness " the approaching cliffs of Albion " in the passage cited above.

The epigram of Jonson to King James, from which the lines above are taken, was written in 1604. The " Panegyric " on the same sovereign's accession, written in the previous year and the earliest extended piece of Jonson's writing in couplets, shows beyond any cavil the beginnings of those qualities which, developed, differentiate the couplet of Dryden and Pope from others' usage of the same measure, and it displays what is more important, a treatment and mode of dealing with material, a diction and style which equally determine its kinship.

We cannot expect the laws which govern organic growth to coincide with those controlling constructive ingenuity; a house is built, a tree grows, and the conscious and self-controlled development of such a man as Jonson is alien to the subtle and harmonious unfolding of a genius like Shakespeare's. What we do find in Jonson's use of the devices of the later classicists is a full recognition of their actual value, and an application of each to the special needs and requirements of the work which he may have in hand. Thus he employed the couplet for epigram and epistle alike, but used it with greater terseness and more in accord with later usage in the former, feeling that fluency and a somewhat negligent manner at times were fitting to epistolary style. The liberality of Jonson's spirit, despite his own strong preferences, caused him to admit into his practice forms which theoretically he disapproved. He had the sanction of Catullus and Tibullus for his lyrics, but he even stooped to write a few sonnets, to bits of pastoral in the prevailing mode like a *Nymph's Passion*, and to *concetti*, like the dainty trifle, *That Women are but Men's Shadows*. This eclecticism of practice in the great classical theorist, combined with the strong influence of Donne's subtle novelty of treatment and the older romantic influence of Spenser, perpetuated in men like Drayton, Drummond and the later Spenserians, delayed the incoming tide of classicism, which setting in, none the less, about the time of the accession of Charles I, became the chief current until after the Restoration, and reached its full when Milton, the last of the Elizabethans, died.

Nothing could more strongly exemplify this eclecticism in the practice of Jonson than the fact that two such diverse men as Robert Herrick and Edmund Waller were alike his poetical "sons." Herrick, the man, has a naïve and engaging personality, which is choice, though not more sterling than the solid worth of Ben Jonson himself; whilst the frank paganism of Herrick, the poet, and his joy in the fleeting beauties of nature are things apart from Jonson's courtly and prevailingly ethical appraisement of the world. Notwithstanding, Herrick had his priceless lyrical gift of Jonson, though he often surpassed his master in it. Unhappily for his fame, he inherited also Jonson's occasional grossness of thought, his fondness for the obscenities of Martial; and he surpassed his master in this as well.

Waller's debt to Jonson is also two-fold: in the lyric,

which he impoverished and conventionalized, and in occasional verse, for which he possessed a peculiar talent, and which he freed of the weight of Jonson's learning, his moral earnestness and strenuousness of style, codifying the result into a system which was to give laws to generations of poets to come. Waller was a man, the essence of whose character was time-serving, to whom ideals were nothing, but to whom immediate worldly success, whether in social life or letters, was much; a man whose very unoriginality and easy adaptability made him precisely the person to fill what has been deftly called the post of " Coryphaeus of the long procession of the commonplace." The instinct of his followers was right in singling Waller out for that position of historical eminence, not because, as a boy, he sat down and deliberately resolved on a new species of poetry, but because he chose out with unerring precision just those qualities of thought, form and diction which appealed to the people of his age, and wrote and re-wrote his poetry in conformity with them. In Carew, Waller found the quintessence of *vers de société*, and " reformed " it of its excessive laces and falling-bands to congruity with the greater formality which governed the costume of the succeeding century. Lastly, in Jonson he found an increasing love of that regularity of rhythm which results from a general correspondence of length of phrase with length of measure, amongst much with which he was in little sympathy, a minute attention to the niceties of expression, a kind of spruce antithetical diction, and a versification of a constructiveness suited to the epigram-matic form in which the thought was often cast. In Sandys, Fairfax, Drummond and some others, he found a smoothness and sweetness of diction, in which these poets departed measurably from their immediate contemporaries and preserved something of the mellifluousness of the Spenserians. With almost feminine tact Waller applied these things to his unoriginal but carefully chosen subject-matter, and in their union wrought his success.

The real value of the following age of repression consisted in its recognition of the place that the understanding must hold — not only in the production of prose — but in the production of every form of enduring art. It endeavored to establish a standard by which to judge, and failed, less because of the inherent weakness of the restrictive ideal, than because the very excess of the imaginative age preceding drove the classicists to a greater recoil and made them content with the correction of abuse instead of solicitous to found their reaction upon a sure foundation. The essential cause of this great change in the literature of England, above all question of foreign origin, precocious inventiveness of individual poets, artificial and " classical heroic couplets," lies in the gradual increase of the understanding as a regulative force in the newer literature, the consequent rise of a well-ordered prose, and the equally consequent suppression for several decades of that free play of the imagination which is the vitalizing atmosphere of poetry.

VI

THE COMMON FOLK OF SHAKESPEARE

SHAKESPEARE . . . seems to me," says Walt Whitman, " of astral genius, first class, entirely fit for feudalism. His contributions, especially to the literature of the passions, are immense, forever dear to humanity — and his name is always to be reverenced in America. But there is much in him ever offensive to democracy. He is not only the tally of feudalism, but I should say Shakespeare is incarnated, uncompromising feudalism in literature." [1]

With such an arraignment of Shakespeare's universality and his sympathy with his fellow men, let us consider the common folk of his plays with a view to discover the poet's actual attitude towards that humbler station in life into which he was himself indisputably born. For our purpose we exclude all personages of rank, all his characters of gentle birth, together with all those, whatever their varying degrees of servitude, who wait upon royalty or form in any wise a part or parcel of the households of great folk. This excludes all of Shakespeare's heroes. It will also exclude Shakespeare's fools, from trifling Launce and delectable Feste to the sad-eyed companion in folly of

[1] *Complete Writings, Prose*, ii, 277.

85

King Lear. And even Falstaff, who was sometime page to Sir Thomas Mowbray and a gentleman, however unlanded, must stand in his dignity without our bounds.

There remain for us, in our middle domain, some three or four score personages who have speaking parts, of a diversity the equal of their betters and inferiors, even although their actual rôles are, for the most part, subordinate. Conveniently to treat so many of the undistinguished, we must group them, a process the more justifiable when we consider that thus we can best ascertain what are really Shakespeare's prejudices and whether they are of class or individual.

The drama by Shakespeare's day had already evolved, or rather created by iteration, several very definite stock personages. One of these is the pedant or schoolmaster, so well known to Italian comedy; and Holofernes, in *Love's Labour's Lost,* with his loquacity, affectation of learning and essential ignorance, is Shakespeare's most certain contribution to the type. As to "the pedant" so nominated in *The Shrew,* this personage is taken over bodily from Gascoigne's *Supposes,* the translation of an Italian play, and performs no "pedantic" function; while Pinch, in *The Errors,* is called in momentarily to exorcise the devil out of half-maddened Antipholus of Ephesus. In the Welshman, Sir Hugh Evans of *The Merry Wives of Windsor,* we modulate, so to speak, from the schoolmaster to the parson, for Evans apparently performed the functions of both. Evans is no fool, however he may have sung to keep up his courage on one memorable occasion, in breaking voice, ungowned and sword in trembling hand, while he awaited the coming of his terrible adversary, the French Doctor Caius, deceived in the meeting, like himself, by a parcel of incorrigible wags.

Shakespeare's curates, parsons and religious folk are many. Of the class of Evans are Sir Nathaniel, in *Love's Labour's Lost* and Sir Oliver Martext in *As You Like It*. Sir Nathaniel is zany to the ponderous folly of Holofernes, he who plays the rôle of " Alisander " to the latter's Judas in the immortal " ostentation, or show, or pageant, or antique of the Nine Worthies "; while our joy in Sir Oliver lies more in his delectable cognomen " Martext " than in the very brief scenes in which he is brought in to " despatch " Touchstone and his Audrey into matrimony under the greenwood tree. The Shakespearean friar is a more important personage, from the plotting, necromantic Home and Southwell in the second part of *Henry VI* to Juliet's Friar Lawrence with his minor counterpart of minor function, Friar Francis in *Much Ado*, and the Duke, disguised as such, in *Measure for Measure*. Whether a matter wholly referable to his sources or not, Shakespeare conceived of the friar of Roman Catholic Verona, Messina or Vienna, in a very different spirit from that in which he represents the small parson, Sir Hugh or Sir Oliver. Friar Francis in *Much Ado* detects the " strange misprision in the two princes " whereby the Lady Hero is slanderously wronged, and it is his prudent advice, which, followed implicitly by the lady and her friends, rights that wrong in the end. The likeness of this function of Friar Lawrence is patent to the most superficial reader; but unhappily for his prudence and his ingenuity, the accident to his messenger, the precipitancy of Romeo, the influence of the very stars is against him and he fails where his brother friar had succeeded. Nowhere in Shakespeare does the clergy function with more dignity than in *Measure for Measure,* whether in the rôle of the chaste and devoted novitiate, Isabella, or in the grave and searching wisdom of the Duke. What Shakespeare's attitude toward formal religion may have been we have little that is definite to go by. Who can doubt that it was he, however, and none other, who paid for the tolling of the great bell of St. Saviours when his brother's body was laid there to rest? And who can question with all his scenes of religious pomp and dignity that Shakespeare recognized, with Wolsey, that all these forms of earthly vanity are

> a burthen
> Too heavy for a man that hopes for heaven?

We may regret that Shakespeare has nowhere exhibited to us, like Chaucer in his "poure Persoun of a toun," his ideal of the cloth. It has been wittily said that it is a credit to human nature that no critic has as yet called Shakespeare a Puritan. It is somewhat less creditable that some have gone about to show him the satirist of Puritanism, especially in Malvolio. It was Jonson, the moralist, who satirized Puritanism, not

88

Shakespeare, whose business was with qualities that differentiate men in the essentials of their natures and in the conduct which these differences entail.

Let us glance next at the physicians of Shakespeare. In Dr. Caius of *The Merry Wives,* although he is boastful of his intelligence from the court, the doctor is lost in the gross wit of the Frenchman's ignorance of English satirized. The apothecary who sells Romeo his death potion, in his " tattered weeds," could assuredly not have been of a profession in which there are no beggars. The father of Helena in *All's Well,* although he left to his daughter the miraculous cure of the King of France by means of his medical secrets, is reported a man of dignity, learning and much experience in his practice. The doctor in *Macbeth* has won the praises of his own jealous profession with the professional aptitude of his comments on the somnambulist symptoms of Lady Macbeth; while the physician, Cornelius, skilled as he is in poisons, honorably deceives the wicked queen of Cymbeline with a sleeping potion instead of the deadly drug which it was her purpose to administer to the unhappy Imogen.

Unlike his contemporary Middleton and some others, Shakespeare does not satirize the profession of the law; and the lawyer, as such, scarcely figures in the plays. At opposite poles, in the plays which have to do with Falstaff, we have Master Shallow " in the county of Gloucester, justice of the peace and ' coram,' " described by Falstaff as " a man made after supper of a cheese-paring . . . for all the world like a forked radish, with a head fantastically carved upon it with a knife." And we have likewise the grave and honorable Chief Justice Gascoigne, whose courage and impartiality in the exercise of his high functions caused the regenerate Prince to choose him for his guide and counsellor on the assumption of his new royal dignities. As to the lesser functionaries of the law, the watchman, the constable and the beadle, Shakespeare exhibits the general free spirit of his time and laughs, as the rest of the world has ever laughed, at the insolence, ineptitude and ignorance of the small man dressed in a little brief authority. It might be argued with some likelihood of success that this is identically the spirit that marks the Sheriff of Nottingham as the butt of the lawless pranks of Robin Hood, the attitude towards constituted authority which combined in the free ranging devils of the old miracle plays the functions of policing the crowd and catering to its merriment. Beyond his designation, "a constable," Dull in *Love's Labour's Lost*, scarcely represents for his class more than his name; and as to Elbow in *Measure for Measure*, his " simplicity " like his malapropisms, seems a faint and colorless repetition of these qualities in the immortal Dogberry. Dogberry is the ubiquitous, inevitable, unescapable man of weight, ponderous alike physically and mentally; for I am persuaded with an old-fashioned American critic, that Dogberry was "of ample size — no small man speaks with sedate gravity. . . . No man of the lean and dwarfish species can assume the tranquil self-consequence of Dogberry. How could a thinly covered soul [exhibit] . . . that calm interior glow, that warm sense, too, of outward security, which so firmly speaks in Dogberry's content and confidence." [2]

Our obvious generalization as to Shakespeare's estimate of the learned professions, then, is this: he found, in all, earnest, honorable and capable men and honored them as such; and he found likewise among them the stupid, the pedantic, the pretentious and the absurd. It was for their follies that he ridiculed them, not because of their class or their station of life.

Of the small gentry of Elizabethan England, Master Ford and Master Page with their two merry wives offer us the best example in comedy. The discordant plans and plots for a provision in life for Mistress Anne Page are in keeping with many a like unconscious parody on the grand alliances of folk of higher station. The foolish Slender, who is likewise a small landed proprietor, is nearer an absolute fool or " natural " than any of Shakespeare's clowns, professional or other, for wit proceeds no more out of him, however he beget wit in others, than it ever comes forth from the mouth of Andrew Aguecheek his cousin-german (so to speak) of Illyria. In Alexander Iden, who meeting with Jack Cade in his Kentish garden, kills him in single fight, we have a serious personage of much Slender's station in life. But Iden has his wits as well as his valor about him and his knighting is his deserved reward. Nearer the soil, if closer to royalty, is the kind-hearted, allegorical-minded king's gardener who apprises the queen of Richard II of that monarch's mischance in falling into the hands of his enemy, victorious Bolingbroke. In the country folk that fill in the background of *As You Like It* and the later acts of *The Winter's Tale*, Shakespeare's English spirit comes into contact with the conventional types of Italian pastoral drama. Corin is the typical shepherdess, beloved but not loving, and Sylvius, the pursuing shepherd unbeloved. But as if to correct an impression so artificial, we have, beside them, William and Audrey, English country folk in name and nature like Costard and Jaquenetta, and in Shakespeare's maturer art, far more redolent of the soil. William, like Slender, and many a man of better station, is a mere natural; but his witlessness is as distinguishable from the folly of the Shakespearean " clown," as his boorishness differs from the literal simplicity of the Shepherd who becomes foster-brother to Perdita in *The Winter's Tale*. Mopsa and Dorcas with their shepherds of the sheep shearing, in these charming comedy scenes, are English country folk; and Autolycus, despite his fine Greek name, is a delightful English rogue and incorrigible vagabond.

And now that we have all but touched the bottom of the Shakespearean social scale, we may note that in Shakespeare poverty does not necessarily make a man vicious; nor does roguery destroy humor in a man or deprive him of his brains. The porter in *Macbeth* is a foul-mouthed drunken lout; the nameless " old man " in the same tragedy is a credulous recorder of marvels. But Adam, the old serving man of Orlando, is faithful almost to death. Dame Quickly of London is a silly old muddlehead, alike innocent of morals and of common sense; and her sister Dame Quickly of Windsor is a shameless go-between and meddler; but the widow, keeper of lodgings for pilgrims in *All's Well*, has a virtuous and honorable disposition. The drawer, Francis, in *Henry IV* " sums up his eloquence in the parcel of a reckoning "; but there is no keener, droller fellow in the world than the grave-digger in *Hamlet*, and it is dubious if for natural parts, however diverted to the " doing " and undoing of his fellows, Autolycus has ever had his equal. Shakespeare's carriers talk of their jades and their packs; his vintners and drawers of their guests and their drinking; his musicians disparage their own skill and have to be coaxed to show it; and his honest botchers, weavers and bricklayers hate learning, and in their rage variously kill a poet and hang a clerk. And curious as all this may appear to him who habitually views the classes below him as merely his servants or the objects of his organized charity, all this — save possibly the homicides — is as true of today as of the age of Shakespeare.

And here perhaps as well as anywhere, we may digress into " the Shakespearean prejudice as to mobs." The mob figures as such conspicuously three times in Shakespeare's plays, in the second part of *King Henry VI*, in *Julius Cæsar*, and in *Coriolanus*. It is represented in all three cases as fickle, turbulent, cruel, foul and possessed of a rude sense of humor; and this last is Shakespeare's — perhaps, more accurately, the Elizabethan — contribution to the picture. It has been well observed that Tudor England presented no precise parallel to the persistent struggle of the Roman plebs against the bulwarks of patrician oligarchy. And it is doubtful if Shakespeare would have sought for such parallels had they existed. In unessentials — and the picture of the mob is such to the dramatic action of these two Roman plays — Shakespeare is always faithful to his sources, and Plutarch's crowd is cruel, seditious, and " contemptibly responsive " to the most obvious blandishments of the demagogue. In the admirable scenes of Jack Cade's rebellion, although the material was nearer home, Shakespeare once more followed his sources, here in Holinshed and Halle. Neither of these worthies comprehended in the slightest degree the actual political issues underlying the Kentishmen's revolt, which historically was as respectable as it was fruitless. But Shakespeare was not seeking historical accuracy, but dramatic effectiveness and fidelity to the observed characteristics of ignorant men escaped from the curb of the law. Shakespeare, as to the mob, was no sociologist, and his yearning for the submerged tenth was not that of many a worthy gentleman of our own time who otherwise misrepresents the unshriven objects of his solicitude. In short a mob was to the unlettered dramatist merely a mob. Man running in packs unbridled by authority was a phenomenon better known to unpoliced Elizabethan England than to us, and Shakespeare found most of his own impressions in this matter to tally remarkably with those of Plutarch and Holinshed.

With Shakespeare's mob we leave the country and meet with the small tradesmen of towns; for even the

Kentish "rabblement" of Jack Cade is represented, like that of ancient Rome, as made up of small trades people — cobblers, butchers, smiths and the like — not folk of the fields. Individually as collectively, Shakespeare has a greater appreciation for the humors of the tailor, the joiner, and the bellows-mender than for his psychology. The drunken tinker of *The Shrew* the author found in his source and, unlike that source, wearied, he dropped his adventures when the play within the play was at an end. The hempen homespuns with the illustrious weaver, Bottom, at their head, repeat in their absurd drama of "Pyramus and Thisbe," a situation already sketched in *Love's Labour's Lost*, one in which the banter and cruel interruption of ungentle gentles evidently reproduces a situation by no means unknown to better actors than Bottom, Flute and Starveling. A kindly spirit speaks in the words of Theseus:

> For never anything can be amiss
> When simpleness and duty tender it;

for truly is he tolerant who can find words of praise for the good intentions of the amateur actor, a being little loved of gods or man. To the professional player, whom he knew better than any other man of art, Shakespeare is courteous and appreciative in the person of Hamlet, and we know from an often-quoted sonnet, how deeply he could feel the degradation which popular contemporary opinion attached to the player's art.

The merchant, in Shakespeare's day, was a far more

dignified person than the mere man of trade. A merchant, it is true, waits with a jeweller, but also with a painter and a poet, in the anteroom of silly, sumptuous Timon. But ordinarily, the merchant is a more dignified person, extending courtesy to strangers, as in *The Comedy of Errors*, taking risks for his merchandise and for himself, as in the case of old Ægeon, in the same play, who has ventured on markets forbidden and is imprisoned for his daring. The most notable Shakespearean merchant is, of course, Antonio, the merchant prince of Venice, an adventurer in the Elizabethan sense into strange markets and a gambler for high commercial stakes. His gravity— or presaging melancholy — befits his dignity, and his generosity to Bassanio, a fellow adventurer (but in more than the Elizabethan sense), is only equalled by his authority among his fellow merchants and his scorn of the unrighteous Jew. Shylock, too, is of the merchant class, but a pariah alike for his race and his practice of usury. But Shylock will take us into precincts irrelevant; for the Jew, whatever your thought of him or mine, is not of the common folk even of Shakespeare.

Next to the merchants come Shakespeare's seamen, the noble-minded Antonio of *Twelfth Night,* Sebastian's friend, the outspoken sea-captain, boatswain and mariners of *The Tempest,* the attendant sailors and fisher folk of *Pericles.* Shakespeare was a landsman; save for an occasional line, his descriptions of the sea, in the richest of all literatures in this respect, are none of them important. The mariner as such he treats with the respect due a person only partially known. With the soldier, in a martial age, Shakespeare was better acquainted and he knew him from the kings and great commanders of the historical plays to such military men of pasteboard and plaster as Parolles, Nym and Pistol. Of Falstaff's levy and his rabble attendants, from Bardolph of the carbuncled nose to the minute page, it may be said that they cut a sorrier figure in France than at the Boarshead in Eastcheap. But Shakespeare's army levied better men than these; the heroic gunners on the walls of Orleans, the brave and capable captains of four kingdoms, Gower, Fluellen, MacMorris, and Jamey in *Henry V*, and the manly English soldiers Bates, Court and Williams. If the refined modern critic, versed in the interminable researches of an incessantly prying age, would learn whether the old dramatist, Shakespeare, had any notions as to the mental processes and moral stability of the common man, let him read and ponder the simple incident of King Henry, incognito, and the soldier Williams with their arguments pro and con as to the responsibility of princes. Williams is the type of the honest, fearless, clearheaded " man in the street " who honors his king, not slavishly because he is a king, but for the qualities that make him kingly, who respects manhood (his own included) above rank and is the more valiant that he knows the cost of valor. There are several well-known tales of military devotion of the soldier, wounded unto death in a quarrel, the righteousness or wrong of which he cares not even to inquire, who dies, blessed and content that he has obeyed, in unquestioning faith, the

august commands of his master. These anecdotes are
not English. Williams is not of this type. His free
soul will challenge his gage in the eye of his prince and
when his heart tells him he is right, let the devil forbid.
Shakespeare, too, knew the common man, and his trust
was in him. Nor did our wise old dramatist, for all his
scenes of the pomp and circumstance of war, forget its
terror, its sorrow and its pathos. In the third part of
Henry VI, that unhappy king is seated alone on the
field of battle as the struggle surges away from him.
And there enters " a son that hath killed his father
dragging in the dead body," and later " a father bearing of his [dead] son." Poignant are the words of
these common men in their common woe, the battle
woe of all ages and all times in the grip of which the
least are as the great and the greatest as the poorest.

In the taverns, the brothels and the jails, Shakespeare found the foulmouthed, the ignorant and the
dishonest and he represented them in all these particulars in a faithful, if at times, forbidding, reality to life.
Moreover, his prejudice against evil is pronounced in
the very repulsiveness of such scenes. He knows that
there are impostors among beggars, that trial by com-
bat is only a somewhat cruder method of getting at the
truth than trial by jury, that there are corrupt and
incompetent magistrates and fools abounding in all
walks of life. Moreover, he depicts in his plays a feudal state of society, for such was English society in his
day. But there is nothing in these honest dramatic
pictures of English life, from the king on his throne to
Abhorson with his headsman's axe, to declare Shake-

speare prejudiced against any class of his fellow countrymen. Wherefore, our obvious generalization as to Shakespeare's attitude toward common folk, whether they be learned or unlearned, is this: he found among them the stupid, the ignorant, the pretentious and the absurd; but he found likewise in each class the earnest, the honorable and capable, and honored each after his kind as such. For their follies he ridiculed them; for their virtues, which he recognized, he loved them, deflecting neither to ridicule nor respect because of station in life.

VII

" SIDNEY'S SISTER, PEMBROKE'S MOTHER "

THE ELIZABETHAN lady of title is our theme, the Elizabethan titled lady in her dignity and power to foster high ideals, in her place as patron and encourager of letters, and in the function by which she added, in the degree of her ability, to the splendid chorus of song, the wealth of drama, and the spirit of the devotion of her time. There were several noble ladies who fulfilled in some sort these conditions. To one or other of them many important contemporary books were inscribed; and, again and again, were they sung and sonneted by the poets. Some are charmingly and allegorically figured by Spenser, with other ladies of Elizabeth's court, in *Colin Clouts Come Home Again*. But without enumeration here, none so completely fulfills our conditions of a patron, a writer herself, and an encourager of letters, as does the sister of the renowned Sir Philip Sidney, Mary Herbert, Countess of Pembroke, who long survived her heroic brother and that grave honorable gentleman, her husband, Henry Herbert, second Earl of Pembroke. It is a commentary on the mutations of time that the two noble sons who were the product of this union, William Herbert, who succeeded to his father's earldom, and his brother, Philip, Earl of Montgomery, are best remembered as the two

noble patrons of the drama to whom was dedicated the
greatest single volume in secular English literature —
the first folio of Shakespeare's collected plays.

But it is not my purpose to tie the reader to a mere
enumeration of the particulars of the life of Mary
Herbert, interesting as many of these particulars are.
Lady Pembroke touched Elizabethan life at many
points, some influentially; and through kinship, association, and patronage, her relations with men of letters in her day were many. She stands, the center, if
not altogether the guiding spirit, of a group of writers,
who, in a sense, maintained the aristocratic and cultivated traditions in which the lamented Sir Philip had
conceived and dreamed of a future for English literature; and it was not her fault that, wanting her brother's brilliant experimental and adventurous temper,
she should have been unable to realize his dreams. It
is, then, not only Lady Pembroke, the collaborator and
reviser of the *Arcadia*, the sharer in her brother's
literary plans and aspirations that shall concern us;
but the Lady Pembroke whose patronage sustained the
literary efforts of men like Breton and Daniel, next to
Spenser and alongside of Drayton, quite the most popular poet of his day; the Lady Pembroke whose example in the translation of contemporary French tragedy
begot a little group of dramas in protest against the
amateurishness of the contemporary London stage and
beguiled even so successful a playwright as Thomas
Kyd, the author of the enormously popular *Spanish
Tragedy*, into experiment in the manner of ancient
and sanctioned usage.

It is a mistake into which none will fall who know somewhat of this old age, to think that the position of women in Tudor times was degraded. It was Samuel Johnson, not Ben Jonson, who, hearing of the extraordinary circumstances that a certain young gentlewoman had become quite proficient in Greek, likened such an accomplishment in a woman to " the curiosity of a dog dancing in a doublet." In point of fact the position and education of women deteriorated steadily from the accession of the Stuarts. But, much in contrast, in the reign of Henry VIII, women of rank and station received a remarkably thorough training, in which such accomplishments as an ability to dance a galliard, to sing madrigals at sight, and perform pavanes and corantoes on the virginals by no means usurped the entire place of a rigorous reading of the classics, Greek as well as Latin, and a current conversancy with French and Italian, and even at times with " High Almain," delectable term for a language so guttural as German. The rigors of the education to which unhappy Lady Jane Grey was subjected are well known and need not be repeated. Queen Elizabeth was not only an accomplished linguist, as the accounts of many a carefully unpremeditated speech of hers in Latin and other foreign languages go to show; she was likewise an exquisite penwoman, and was as proud of the calligraphy of her writings as she was of their graceful ceremoniousness. In a late book on Queen Elizabeth,[1] which by the way quite vindicates the great queen of many of the lingering aspersions on her mem-

[1] J. C. Chamberlin, *The Private Character of Queen Elizabeth*, 1922.

ory, you can see facsimile reproductions of her handwriting and of letters the cleverness and perspicacity
of which were equalled by no man of her time or any
other. And while the Queen may have been distinguished in her accomplishments according to her station, she was by no means alone among the clever
women of her England.

From quite another point of view, I should advise
him who would know the Elizabethan woman to read
her in the literature of her age. While much of the
adulation to which she was subjected rings strange and
discordant now — because we pay our adulation in
other coin — I find a sincerity, take it all in all, in the
eulogistic poetry of the older days which I do not find
later. If any modern young woman shall fire with in-
dignation at the patient Griseldas of our older literature and the rampant shrews, tamed to eat out of hand
by the prowess of man, I advise that she read Fletcher's
comedy of *The Tamer Tamed,* the return match, so to
speak, in which Maria, immortal second wife of Petruchio, triumphantly vindicates her sex. And if doubt
still persists, make acquaintance with the many Elizabethan leading ladies — shall we call them? — who
take life and fate into their own hands and, compe-
tently playing the game, worst what is veritably the
weaker sex in every encounter. To be quite serious, it
was not in idle compliment that Ruskin wrote, in a
famous and familiar passage:

Shakespeare has no heroes; — he has only heroines. . . . The
castastrophe of every play is caused always by the folly or fault

of a man; the redemption, if there be any, by the wisdom and
virtue of a woman, and failing that, there is none.

There is in Shakespeare no cheap gallantry. His is a
faithful replica of the Elizabethan man and woman in
the life that he knew so well and reproduced so unerringly. There were three things which healthy Elizabethan society did not know; and these are gallantry,
sentimentalism, and cynicism: all of this affects our
portraiture of the Elizabethan woman.

When I say that gallantry was unknown to the Elizabethans, perhaps I say too much. It is the cheap and
degenerate gallantry of the days of the Restoration,
to be sure, that I have in mind, when every man was
Nimrod and every woman potentially game of the
chase. This was not Elizabethan gallantry, however
we recall Sir Walter Raleigh, the puddle, her majesty,
and the velvet cloak. The gallantry that identified al-
legiance to an incomparable sovereign, respect for
womanhood, and the protecting spirit which comes to
the physically strong at the thought of the weak —
such gallantry there was; and it was an admirable
union this, begetting the splendid patriotism that rose
to the defeat of the Spanish Armada and other heroic
deeds by land and sea. But by my two other denials, I
stand. There is not a sentimental passage in all
Shakespeare, nor yet in Dekker nor Jonson; we must
wait until Fletcher and Ford for that. People were too
busy, too adventurous, too vividly alive in this period of the adolescence of the English race to turn
their thoughts back upon their inner consciousness in
pity and mawkish study of the ego. Cynicism was

sooner to come, but in Elizabeth's own lifetime as yet
there was little of it. Jaques, pondering in the Forest
of Arden, is a very gentle cynic; even Hamlet is no real
misanthrope, however his world is out of joint. For
cynicism, too, we must pass into the reign of James
and wait for the full influence of that strange and enigmatic poet, Donne. There are advantages in growing
up in a world in which our eyes may still maintain that
openness to direct impressions which belongs to childhood, in which their lids have not been contracted by
too great a glare of the world to a cynical scrutiny of
the conduct of others or narrowed to that absorbing
and belittling self-consciousness which we call sentimentalism.

Freedom from all this was Lady Mary's. Born the
daughter of Sir Henry Sidney and Mary Dudley, sister
of the famous Earl of Leicester, Mary Sidney's childhood combined the advantages of noble ancestry with
comparative poverty; for Sir Henry was a man of little wealth and too honest, despite several ambassador-
ships and the governorship, successively of Ireland and
Wales, to amass a fortune. At beautiful Penshurst,
in Kent, and at picturesque Ludlow Castle, on the
marches of Wales, the young Sidneys passed their
childhood, Philip, Robert, Mary, and a younger sister
who died early; and, although her marriage with the
Earl of Pembroke, a man much her senior and not un-
scarred with political intrigue, was made by high con-
tracting parties who little consulted the inclinations of
the lady, the union turned out remarkably happy.
Scrutiny of the acquisitive purposes and intricate ne-

gotiations of Elizabethan marriages in high life is not altogether edifying. Mammon largely entered into them; though notwithstanding, a cynic might perhaps remark that the god of gold was often as benign a sovereign in these cases as the giddy young bowman whom he supplanted. The tastes of the earl and his young countess were much in accord. Neither cared for the glitter of the court, and they joined in their stately Baynard's Castle, on what is now the Thames Embankment, and at their seat at Wilton, in charitable offices and in the patronage of scholarship and religion. We hear of substantial gifts and pensions not only to retainers such as the poet Samuel Daniel, but for the maintenance at the universities on the Pembroke bounty of promising young men like Philip Massinger, later to become a notable dramatic poet. Meres compares Lady Pembroke to Octavia, sister of Augustus and patron of Vergil; and Nash declares that " arts do adorn [her] as a second Minerva, and our poets extol her as the patron of their inventions." In this Lady Pembroke was but following the example of " her own Philip," as she called her brother, who had aided the education of more than one who was needy, and had become, by the time of his death, despite the fact that he was far from rich, the all but universal patron of science and letters.

At the mention of the name of Philip Sidney, the lover of literature recalls his exquisite sequence of sonnets, *Astrophel and Stella*, and the transfer in them of Petrarchan lyricism to the romantic circumstances of the poet's own love story. The historian will remember the important services of Sir Philip abroad and the golden opinions which his gracious personality gathered at every hand for his judgment, his courtesy, and his competency in scholarship and statecraft. No truer touchstone of this young idol of his time, for whose untimely death all England mourned, could we find than the often repeated tale of his denial of the draught of water, brought him as he lay mortally wounded, because he saw in a common soldier, even more grievously hurt than himself, a need greater than his own. Sidney, with all his gentleness, was bold even to the criticism of his sovereign; and when the young Earl of Oxford, however his superior in rank, had the impertinence, in a quarrel on the tennis court, to call Sir Philip " a puppy," that fiery young gentleman had to be enjoined by the royal command to keep the peace and to go into exile from court until he could command his temper. It was at Wilton, not Penshurst, while under the queen's displeasure, that Sir Philip wrote *The Countess of Pembroke's Arcadia*, as he called his heroic romance, because it was inspired by her ladyship and owed more, he would have said, to that inspiration and her suggestion than to any inventiveness of his own. It is a charming picture this of the young brother and sister, pacing the formal knotted Elizabethan gardens or sitting in the shade of leafy beeches, and yet afar off in their fresh imaginative minds among the unrealities of Arcadian adventure, delighting in the ingenuities of invention and in the flowery and fervid poetical expression in which they clothed their fantastic thoughts. The scholar will tell you that the

Arcadia was borrowed ultimately from the Greek romances and point you parallels in Montemayor and Sannazaro; and the precisian will explain that its luxuriant prose is a usurpation by that useful everyday medium of the functions of poetry. Of course such a romance as this was never finished. And there was no reason in the world why it ever should be. It straggles on with the curves, the new directions, the involutions, and the complexities of a beautiful, flowering vine. You or I might bind up a fallen spray here or twist back an exuberant shoot; but the shears of criticism only lop its foliage and its blossoms to leave behind a twisted and contorted stalk.

Neither the *Arcadia* nor any other writing of Sidney was printed in his lifetime. Such a thing was quite unthinkable in a gentleman of his station; and it has been said that a suggestion to Sir Philip that one of his passionate sonnets should appear in print might have cost the impertinent suggester precipitation down a flight of stairs. The lyrics which Sidney wrote he regarded as purely a private affair; and however well the select circle of the court might know by way of gossip, or in sympathy perhaps, of his attachment for Lady Rich, the Stella of his sonnets, the matter was no business of a reading public. The degree to which any of the Elizabethan sequences of sonnets is to be conceived of as actually autobiographical, remains one of the moot questions of modern scholarship. The determination of the point at which Sidney's poetry lies between the extremes of a story little to his credit and a

species of Anglicized Petrarchanism utterly unauto-
biographical, happily does not concern us here.

On Sidney's death, Lady Pembroke cherished his
manuscripts, we may feel sure, with the same wealth of
sisterly affection which she had bestowed upon him
living. Much of his poetry now came indirectly and
surreptitiously into print, manuscripts being readily
procurable; for few about the cultivated and gallant
court of Elizabeth who cared for poetry, would lose an
opportunity to transcribe verses of the celebrated Sir
Philip into the commonplace-books, as they were
called, which everyone pretending to culture habitually kept. In 1596, therefore, the Countess procured
the publication of the *Arcadia* in what has now become
for bibliophiles, as well as lovers of literature, a precious little quarto; and she lived to see five more editions follow. The question of Lady Pembroke's personal share in the *Arcadia* is set forth, we may well
believe faithfully, in the printer's address to the reader,
prefixed to a late folio edition in which we read:

It moved that noble lady to whose honor consecrated, to whose
protection it was committed, to take in hand the wiping away
those spots wherewith the beauties thereof were unworthily blem-
ished. But, as often repairing a ruinous house, the mending of
some old part occasioneth the making of some new; so here her
honorable labor, began in correcting the faults, ended in supply-
ing the defects; by the view of what was ill done, guided to the
consideration of what was not done. . . . It is now by more
than one interest *The Countess of Pembroke's Arcadia;* done, as
it was, for her; as it is by her. Neither shall these pains be the
last (if no unexpected accident cut off her determination) which

the everlasting love of her excellent brother will make her consecrate to his memory.

Turning now to other matters, there is a well known passage in Sir Philip Sidney's famous little tract, *The Defense of Poesy*, in which he praises that stiff and amateurish production, *Gorboduc*, the earliest English tragedy of regular construction, and passes severe strictures on the popular stage for its want of decorum and its failure to preserve the classical unities. Sidney was writing about 1582; *Gorboduc* was already twenty years old, as it had been acted before Elizabeth by students of the Inner Temple two years before the birth of Shakespeare. Inconsiderate comment on Sidney still sometimes inquires: Why was that keen mind oblivious to the glories of Elizabethan literature and drama? And the obvious answer is that in 1582 there were as yet few such glories; Marlowe, Kyd, to say nothing of Shakespeare, all were yet to come. Sidney was dead in 1586; the earliest successes of the popular tragic stage were just then beginning; even the vogue of Lyly and Spenser's greater fame, neither was as yet. With all his conservative and aristocratic tastes, Sidney was an experimentalist in literature, however he believed that the future of English poetry and drama lay less in the affectation of mere novelty than in an effort to try out every lead. Sidney had attempted classical meters in English; he had imitated Italian madrigals, sestinas, terza rima, ottava rima, and what not; and he believed implicitly, as we have just seen, in the acceptance of classical usages for the cultivated drama of school and court which he looked forward hopefully to see develop in England, as it had already developed in Italy and France. Wherefore when we find the Countess of Pembroke translating a tragedy of French Robert Garnier, on Antony, preserving its severe Senecan features, we recognize at once that her ladyship was only attempting to sustain the avowed ideals of her brother, although they were now at least a generation out of date. The Countess of Pembroke's *Antonie* is no unusual specimen of its dreary kind; the interesting thing is that it should have heralded, at so late a date, a group of like plays, all of them penned by courtly writers of the little circle which surrounded her ladyship: Daniel, her poet; Kyd, who dedicated his translation of Garnier's *Cornelia* to her; Fulke Greville, her brother's boyhood friend and biographer; each attempted this stilted tragic art, possibly less in any conscious rivalry of the stage of Marlowe and Shakespeare than in protest against its discard of their beloved classical usages and examples; for few, if any, of these productions were acted, despite the genuine poetic value of several of them. It speaks volumes for the influence of Lady Pembroke and the persistency of the Sidnean ideals of literary art that this group of courtly and reactionary tastes should have written, tied to the ancients at a time so late. Had their influence prevailed, as similar influences continued to prevail in France, our drama might now chronicle an English Corneille and Racine in place of Shakespeare, Jonson, and Fletcher.

There are other things to show how assiduously Lady Pembroke trod in the footsteps of her brother.

A pleasing chapter in the annals of Elizabeth tells of her royal progresses, as they were called, in season of fine weather, from noble house to noble house of her liege subjects. There could be, of course, no greater honor than this, the entertainment of the queen. And some there were who essayed it to the impoverishment of their fortunes; for Elizabeth was possessed of little appreciation of the blessedness of the giver. The elaboration of some of these royal entertainments was extraordinary; and her majesty seems never to have wearied of speeches of welcome, decorative pageantry, allegorical tableaux, and dramatic performances of every conceivable variety. As long ago as 1578, Sidney had devised for his uncle Leicester's entertainment of Elizabeth at Wansted Garden, the earl's seat in Waltham Forest, a lively little pastoral scene, *The Lady of May;* and three years later he and his friend, Fulke Greville, were conspicuous participants in a sumptuous mock tournament, likewise provided for the royal pleasure. Towards the end of 1599, it appears that the Countess of Pembroke had the honor of becoming the Queen's hostess on her majesty's visit into Wiltshire. Her ladyship, on this occasion, followed once more her brother's lead, writing with her own hand *A Pastoral Dialogue in Praise of Astrea* — who is Elizabeth of course — in which, to be quite frank, neither the form, by this time quite outworn, nor the quality of its poetical expression successfully sustained the undoubted loyalty which prompted the effort.

In the matter of minor poetry, I am not altogether

sure that a fellow-feeling always makes us wondrous kind; although our own contemporary minor poets do seem to tend to a certain flocking together in small groups, much sustained, we may well believe, by mutual admiration. However, as to Lady Pembroke, many were the minor poets who dedicated their efforts to her kindly encouragement. Abraham Fraunce, belated producer of that abomination, English hexameters; Charles Fitzgeoffrey, Latin epigrammatist; Davies of Hereford, mild, effusive satirist; Dr. Moffatt, who wrote a "poem" on the silkworm; Henry Lok, unrepentant, after the perpetration of several hundred devotional sonnets characterized solely by piety: these are some of them. Donne, the eminent Dean of Saint Paul's, was the personal friend of the countess and wrote to her several fine occasional poems. Nicholas Breton, graceful pastoralist, dedicated several of his verse pamphlets to her. But it was Samuel Daniel who was, by all odds, the most complete and typical outcome of the Sidney-Pembroke circle. Tutor to the nobility, especially to several noble ladies, a courtier, conservative, reticent, well bred, accomplished, Daniel represents in his smooth and uniformly adequate poetry the development which Sidney had presaged for the art he so loved. It was Daniel who earned from his contemporaries the adjective "well-languaged," from the purity and grace of his diction; and as we read his delicately wrought sonnets, his graceful pastorals, his carefully modelled classic drama and grave occasional poetry, we recognize in him the very incarnation of the Sidnean spirit.

It has been said that in a wider sense the literary associations of the Herberts may be extended to include practically every important book in general literature published in England from Spenser's *Faery Queen* to Milton's *Comus;* and in that wider range must not be forgotten the cultivated Lady Magdalen Herbert, mother of three notable sons: the conceited poet autobiographist, Lord Herbert of Cherbury, Sir Henry Herbert, busy Master of the Revels and licenser of plays, and the holy poet, George Herbert, whose beautiful devotional poetry still finds place in the hearts of the devout. Lady Magdalen Herbert was the friend and correspondent of Dr. Donne when he was Dean of St. Paul's, and, left a widow early, devoted herself to the education of her younger sons, residing the while at Cambridge for the purpose, and mingling in learned as well as noble circles. Her husband was a kinsman of the Pembrokes, however in a younger branch of the Herberts.

Let us now turn back to William Herbert, the Pembroke of our title and first of the two noble dedicatees of the famous first folio edition of the plays of Shakespeare. An earlier association of these two names than this has been sought in the attempt to identify his lordship with the mysterious " Mr. W. H." who figures as " the only begetter " in the cabalistic dedication of the *Sonnets* of Shakespeare. But his lordship was known before his father's death as "Lord Herbert" and, before we accept this identification, it is to be remembered that there might be citation before Star Chamber with pains and penalties to such as would dare so to

derogate, especially in print, from the proper title of
the son of a peer. Moreover, if we accept the notion
that "Mr. W. H." was really William, Lord Herbert,
Shakespeare, at any reasonable date for the writing of
the *Sonnets,* must be represented as urging a boy of
fourteen or fifteen to hasten his marriage and settle-
ment in life, an advocacy of early wedlock outstripping
even the Shakespearean biographical example.

Returning to the dedication of the first folio of
Shakespeare's plays, we are on more certain ground.
As we turn to the familiar words of the epistle dedicatory, we are at once given pause at the obsequious-
ness, if not the the absolute servility, of its tone. Their
lordships, Pembroke and Montgomery, are addressed
in words to which we can only apply the term of worship. There is "rashness" and "fear" in the enterprise and "a kind of religious address," to quote the
actual words, though we are assured that "the
meanest of things are made more precious when they
are dedicated to temples." But we learn, too, that
their lordships had been "pleased to consider these
trifles" — such as *Hamlet, Lear,* and *Macbeth* —
"somewhat;" and that "so much were your lordships'
likings of their several parts when they were acted, as
(that) before they were published, the volume asked to
be yours." The age had proceeded far in drama as
contrasted with the frigidities of Lady Pembroke's
translations; and her sons in their appreciation clearly
had advanced with the age. It is good to know that
these noble lords had "prosecuted with favor," as the
quaint phrase goes, the dramatist whose genius more

than anything else has made their age and language famous; and thus to realize how the whirligig of time has wrought in his revenges. As we read these old dedications with their prostrations of talent and even genius before rank, we may console ourselves that many an insolent dedicatee has now only this slender claim on remembrance. After all, however, we may make too much of all this. The language of eulogy, of compliment and adulation is not unlike fashionable attire, a thing elegant and approved in its time; but quaint to the degree of the ridiculous ever after.

One great poet seems not to have been drawn into the Sidnean circle until late. And strange to say this was Ben Jonson to whom has been attributed, though inaccurately, the fine epitaph on the Countess of Pembroke, a line of which has served for the title of this paper. Jonson, with all his love of learning and with the host of his titled friends, was in many respects antithetical to the Sidnean ideals. Where Sidney, as with respect to the ancients, had been imitative and experimental, Jonson was assimilative and made what he abundantly borrowed his own. Sidney's attitude was that of the enthusiastic amateur; Jonson's that of the assiduous scholar to whom learning had become a vocation. As to Daniel, Jonson had recognized almost from the first, in Daniel's Italianate poetry and manner of the courtier-retainer, an object marked for the bolts of his ridicule. However, there seems little question that when the printers and the actor friends of Shakespeare were projecting the publication of his collected plays, it was Jonson whom they procured to write this very dedication of which I have just spoken, together with the precious " address to the reader " and other prefatory matter. Nor was this unnatural. Jonson had already dedicated " the ripest of my studies," as he called his *Epigrams,* to William, Earl of Pembroke. One of the epigrams is addressed to his lordship, and a fine poem of Jonson's *Forest* dilates on the hospitality and rural delights of Penshurst, in these later days of King James the seat of Robert, Earl of Leicester, the brother of Sidney. Both the hospitality and the delights of Penshurst, we have reason to know, Jonson had more than once enjoyed. But this intimacy was with a younger generation than that of our Countess of Pembroke.

Her ladyship survived to the year 1621; and her later literary activities were devoted to charitable offices and religious exercises. Lady Pembroke had long since translated from the French of her brother's friend, Plessis de Mornay, her *Discourse of Life and Death;* and she now gave her attention to the revision and completion of a translation of the *Psalms,* long ago begun by Sir Philip. This version resisted print until just a hundred years ago, when a limited edition was published by a bibliophile, one of the laborious tribe that spare us none of the neglected leavings of genius. But the *Psalms* of the Sidneys had existed during all these years in several manuscript copies, especially in private hands, and their translation appears to have been employed in several noble families for private worship in preference to the plebeian version in print of Sternhold and Hopkins: a pretty commentary, by the way, on class consciousness carried into poetry and devotion. As to the translation of the *Psalms* in these old times, I should like, on proof, to chronicle the only prince, the single nobleman, the one literary lady or everyday poet who did not, at one time or another, translate at least three or four of the *Psalms of David*. Such a man or woman would be conspicuous in his or her time. King James translated psalms, and Queen Elizabeth, of course; and so, by the way, did my Lord Bacon, and very badly, that being his chief claim to a place among poets. To return to Lady Pembroke, I do not really know the poetical value of her translation of the *Psalms*. In these matters I confess that, like Charles Lamb with respect to the soliloquy, "To be or not to be," from very familiarity, I do not know whether this is good, bad, or indifferent poetry. An excellent old writer in the *Gentleman's Magazine*, some eighty years ago, declared of Lady Pembroke's efforts in this kind: "For melodious cadence, variety of metre, and faithfulness of translation, they will hardly be found to be equalled by any other English version." Let us gallantly, or shall I say charitably, let it go at that.

The ordinary cultivated lover of English poetry, asked to name the best epitaph, not in the English language perhaps, but at least in our elder age, would doubtless reply: "Why, Jonson's epitaph about 'Sidney's sister, Pembroke's mother,' to be sure." And he would quote:

> Underneath this marble hearse,
> Lies the subject of all verse,

"SIDNEY'S SISTER, PEMBROKE'S MOTHER"

Sidney's sister, Pembroke's mother;
Death, ere thou hast slain another
Wise and fair and good as she,
Time shall throw a dart at thee.

Now these famous lines occur in none of Ben Jonson's works until they were included by Whalley in his edition of that poet, on the principle that they are so good that nobody but Jonson could possibly have written them. This highly scientific method of the attribution of authorship is not unknown to our own enlightened times. Although it is not to be denied that the epigram is in Jonson's mode; on the other hand these lines do occur in a holographic manuscript volume of William Browne of Tavistock, an excellent poet who enjoyed the intimacy of the Earl of Pembroke, the countess's son; and he very well may have written them. Another stanza is sometimes added, surmised to be the addition of Pembroke himself. I shall not quote these verses to show how bad they are, although that might be a reason for quoting them. If they were written in lieu of the monument which the earl had promised to the memory of Lady Pembroke in Salisbury Cathedral where she was interred, a monument never erected, then these verses are but a poor recompense for so unfilial a neglect.

It must not be supposed that Lady Pembroke was without rivals in her patronage of the poets. An even more universal patroness of learning was Lucy Farington, for the celebration of whose marriage at court with Edward Russell, Earl of Bedford, in 1594, there are some who think that Shakespeare wrote *A Mid-*

summer Night's Dream. It was to Lady Bedford that Ben Jonson paid, in one of his epigrams, quite the finest compliment to perfect womanhood in the language. As this epigram sets forth the contemporary ideal of the patroness of letters as well, I shall make no apology for quoting it. It runs:

> This morning, timely rapt with holy fire,
> I thought to form unto my zealous Muse,
> What kind of creature I could most desire
> To honor, serve, and love, as poets use.
> I meant to make her fair and free and wise,
> Of greatest blood, and yet more good than great,
> I meant the day-star should not brighter rise,
> Nor lend like influence from his lucent seat.
> I meant she should be courteous, facile, sweet,
> Hating that solemn vice of greatness, pride;
> I meant each softest virtue, there should meet,
> Fit in that softer bosom to reside.
> Only a learned and a manly soul
> I purposed her; that should with even powers,
> The rock, the spindle, and the shears control
> Of destiny; and to spin her own free hours.
> Such when I meant to fain and wished to see,
> My Muse bade, " Bedford write," and *that* was she.

Besides her taste in poetry, Lady Bedford was reported to have been an authority on "ancient medals," which I take it means numismatics. She had, too, the good sense to leave no verse of her own writing behind to be damned with faint praise in a generation which had forgotten her. A like restraint cannot be claimed for Lady Mary Wroth. As the daughter of Sidney's brother, Robert, she added to a sympathetic patronage of contemporary literature an ambition to contribute to it. This she at last satisfied in *The Countess of Montgomery's Urania,* as she called her endeavor to emulate the style and the story of her uncle's *Arcadia.* The title of *Urania* sets forth with much detail her ladyship's relations to the Sidneys and the Pembrokes, the "Countess" being Susan, Countess of Montgomery, Lady Wroth's cousin, also not unsung by poets. There seems to have been some notion at the time that *Urania* reflected certain amorous adventures, not without a basis in fact, in the court of King James. If true, in this as in any real genius, Lady Mary's romance differs widely from that of her uncle Sidney. She was Jonson's special patron. To her he dedicated his famous play, *The Alchemist,* besides writing several eulogistic poems in her name. Still nearer to Sidney was Elizabeth, Countess of Rutland, his only daughter. There is a fine epistle by Jonson, once more, to this lady in which he asks,

> What sin 'gainst your great father's spirit
> Were it to think that you should not inherit
> His love unto the Muses, when his skill
> Almost you have, or may have, when you will?

It does not appear that Lady Rutland seriously exercised her inherited talents. Jonson was a consummate courtier, yet his verses to these fine ladies, with all their compliments and charming things well put, are often serious and always self-respecting.

And Jonson in this, as in so much more, was the measure of his time, however it had fallen away somewhat from the simpler days of his childhood. In Elizabeth's age we find, take it all in all, a fine sense of the obligations of station in this matter of the patronage of letters as well as in the more common associations of life. There is this to be said for the feudal relations of society, they suppress, but they also sustain; and the link that binds their mutual obligations is in its essence a personal one. Where these relations have been superseded by those which are determined almost wholly, as now, by barter and sale, the personal element is reduced to a minimum and the obligations of duty, generosity, and charity all but disappear. The cultivated Elizabethan women who encouraged letters, graciously received the praises of poets, and dabbled in writing, as did their lords and husbands, and with about equal success, could little have dreamed of such a person, for example, as scandalous Mistress Aphra Behn of Restoration times, the first English professional literary woman, who wrote plays, poetry, fiction with the swagger and abandon of a man, and eked out a precarious and checkered career by serving her sovereign as an informer and a spy. Even Mrs. Katherine Philips, the Matchless Orinda, as she was dubbed by her admiring friends, Aphra's contemporaries, with her salon on the borders of Wales, poetizing to an admiring group of stiffly proper people, who masqueraded in the disguises of classical names and tried to behave as nearly as possible like the characters of Honoré D'Urfée's graceful and interminable romance, *L'Astrée*, even this Matchless Orinda would sorely have puzzled my Lady Pembroke. A more comprehensible lady who intervened between these subjects of Elizabeth and of Charles II, was Margaret Cavendish, Duchess of Newcastle, who with the Duke, her husband, delighted in generous benefactions to the old Jonson in the latter years of his life. This interesting couple were not only munificent patrons of literature both before and after the Restoration, but both were ambitious of literary fame. While the Duke appropriately wrote chiefly on horsemanship and fencing, her grace was much addicted to drama. Her comedies, which are veritable curiosities, if little more, show every here and there the guidance of a firmer hand. Even in the world of patronage there must be some compensations, some services rendered; and with the picture of her handsome, imperative, stage-struck grace, haughtily submitting her verbose and ill-considered scenes to the scrutiny of the greatest dramatic poet of his time, habitually testy, but now patient if harassed, we may leave a topic which has strayed out of its bounds.

I am not quite sure that it is fitting to draw a moral to adorn my tale. We are told in these late days with somewhat wearisome repetition that woman has at last "arrived," and that she has come to stay. I do not question woman's arrival; biologically, if not mythologically, she may well have arrived before man. And for my part I sincerely hope that she may be prevailed upon to stay. In education I have never been able to see any good reason why opportunities should be extended to one sex to the exclusion or limitation of the other. And this does not raise the nice question as to whether the same education, in the same subjects, in the same place, and at the same time, is the only solution of a troublesome problem. As to literature, too, it is no longer a marvel that a woman should write; the marvel is that there are still men left among the poets, the novelists, essayists, editors, and soon perhaps it will be legislators, and let us hope a stateswoman or so as well. And yet, if we are not to be content merely with swarming mediocrity in which, whether the work be that of man, woman, or child, assuredly is of little moment, can we not rise to a higher standard and leave out, at least in this matter of the arts, this oppressive, this ubiquitous question of sex? Moreover, need we all, save for the personal pleasure that is in it, need we all be creative? Is there not a function as necessary in its way to the healthy flourishing of literature, music, and art, all but as important as creation itself? It is a wise dispensation that where there is one born poet there are a hundred who can respond to the thought, the beauty, the significance which he has created, a thousand who may ultimately be reached through that imitative faculty which causes us to like to walk in the wake of those who lead. It is this function of those who lead, whether man or woman, which I want to emphasize in conclusion. We cannot all be gracious patrons like Lady Pembroke, receiving homage and bestowing bounty; but we can cultivate our taste, refine our feelings, and so guide our appreciation that we can radiate helpfulness and encourage good art in our power to distinguish it. We can do more; like the Lady Mary, we can live by a great tradition — even granting that hers was a little outworn. Each can raise to himself or herself a standard of taste, an ideal as to sound art and, proving true to it, aid in the measure of his or her ability in a wider diffusion of veritable culture. And woman, in the degree of her more delicate perceptions, her sounder instincts, her more exalted ideals, may remain, let us hope, after all, for the future as she has been heretofore, the truest patron of poetry and the arts.

VIII

SHAKESPEARE AND THE LAW

A RECENT BROCHURE lies before me which revives this interesting topic with much legal acumen and, what is better, with as much common sense.[1] The author is an English barrister and a well-known expresser of doubts, in several pamphlets, concerning much that is usually accepted about Shakespeare. But he follows no beaten track even in his agnosticism and is not unaware of the bearings of Shakespeare's knowledge of the law on that tedious but persistent triviality, the query " Who wrote Shakespeare's plays for him? "

A familiar old book of much repute in its day was Lord Campbell's *Shakespeare's Legal Acquirements*. In it the learned Chancellor contended with eloquence, it will be remembered, that Shakespeare was possessed of " a deep technical knowledge of the law," together with " an easy familiarity with some of the most abstruse proceedings of English jurisprudence." This was in 1859; and it seems that his Lordship was considerably in debt to a smaller and less celebrated work by William Lowes Rushton, barrister of Gray's Inn, entitled *Shakespeare as a Lawyer*, which had ap-

[1] *Shakespeare's Law*, by Sir George Greenwood, 1920.

peared in the previous year, although his Lordship omitted any acknowledgment of this, his humble predecessor. This matter of precedence is of little importance now. Subsequently Rushton published two other works on this topic; both are worthy of study.[2] Rushton makes a nice point when he reminds readers that even Lord Campbell is guilty of some slips in the law: wherefore why condemn Shakespeare, who at least was not a Lord Chancellor?

As far back as 1821, Malone, one of the ablest of Shakespeare critics, pronounced that the poet's "knowledge and application of legal terms . . . has the appearance of technical skill"; whilst our own eminent American Shakespearean, Richard Grant White, like Malone a lawyer, declared that "legal phrases flow from Shakespeare's pen as part of his vocabulary and parcel of his thoughts." Other witnesses are called, legal and lay; among them, the distinguished editor of Shakespeare, George Steevens, his bibliographers, the Cowden Clarkes, Professor Churton Collins and several Baconians, though these latter, as interested witnesses, are perhaps better ruled out of court.

A suggestive change of view as to Shakespeare's legal accuracy is that of the late Sir Sidney Lee. In an earlier edition, that of 1899, Sir Sidney simply followed earlier tradition, accepting "Shakespeare's accurate use of legal terms" without further question. In the revision of his *Life* in 1915 "the poet's legal

2 *Shakespeare's Testamentary Language* (1869) and *Shakespeare's Legal Maxims* (1870).

knowledge" becomes " a mingled skein of accuracy and inaccuracy and the errors are far too numerous and important to justify, on sober inquiry, the plea of technical experience:" It is perhaps pertinent to interpolate here that Sir Sidney Lee's *Life of Shakespeare* was a good piece of biographical gathering, as first published, which has been somewhat spoiled by the overlaying of additional information as it has subsequently arisen at the expense of form and sometimes of consistency. Sir George certainly seems here to have put his finger on a case in point; and a footnote of Sir Sidney's referring to a book by Charles Allen [3] of Boston makes clear the source of Sir Sidney's suddenly developed skepticism as to Shakespeare's legal knowledge. The sixth chapter of Mr. Allen's book is entitled " Bad Law in Shakespeare." It is made up of a series of objections to the use of certain legal terms, certain legal procedures and other like matters, so far as I can personally see, largely on the basis that these things do not comport with our contemporary definitions, our present practices and our American — or at least English — statutes of to-day. For example, Mr. Allen objects to the sworn agreement of the young courtiers with their king, in *Love's Labour's Lost:*

> To keep those *statutes*
> That are recorded in this schedule here,

because " a statute," he informs us, " imports a legislative act," and there was none such here. Apparently he is unaware of the familiar " Statutes Merchant,"

[3] *Notes on the Bacon-Shakespeare Question,* (1900).

"Statutes Staple," in which the word equals " rule " or " regulation," as Sir George happily reminds him. Again, Mr. Allen comments seriously on the provision of the will of Portia's father, by which each suitor submits to the test of the caskets, and, failing, must renounce wedlock. " This testamentary prohibition in restraint of marriage, with no means of enforcing it, would seem to have been the invention of a story-teller rather than a lawyer," comments Mr. Allen. Precisely. And still again he quite as solemnly suggests that conduct such as Portia's in impersonating Doctor Bellario, " if it were possible under our system, would be good ground of disbarment here " to any lawyer, we may assume, a party to it. Portia could scarcely have been disbarred. Apparently they take these matters seriously in Boston. It would be absurd to take up the demolition of objections of this captious and unimaginative kind, did we not keep before us, as does Sir George very pertinently, that the foremost contemporary biographer of Shakespeare has been actually misled by such stuff into the statement: " No judicious reader of *The Merchant of Venice* or *Measure for Measure* can fail to detect a radical unsoundness in Shakespeare's interpretation alike of elementary legal principles and of legal procedure."

Besides the trifles mentioned above and the more important matters involved in the two plays just named, Sir George discusses several other points raised by Mr. Allen and others before him, meeting the issue in some cases, avoiding it in others; for he plainly constitutes himself as of counsel for the defence throughout his pamphlet, howsoever he confesses in the end, *adhuc sub judice lis est.* In *Richard III* Queen Elizabeth [Woodville] asks:

> Tell me, what state, what dignity, what honor
> Canst thou *devise* to any child of mine?

precisely as Celia in *As You Like It,* speaking of her father to Rosalind her cousin, says: "And truly, when he dies, thou shalt be his *heir.*" Now neither "devise" nor "heir" is employed correctly and technically in either of these passages; obviously, because there is no reason on earth — out of the mind of an unimaginative pettifogger — why they should be so employed. Neither Celia in the Forest of Arden nor the queen of Edward IV may be supposed, by the wildest flight of the imagination, to have been learned in the law. These and many similar cases in Shakespeare of careless colloquialisms, where such is the veritable utterance of everyday life, may be set down to the dramatic instinct of the poet. They have no reference whatever to "good law" or "bad."

Another group of Shakespearean examples of law and legal procedures is referable to the poet's sources. One of the peculiarly English traits of Shakespeare is the manner in which he uses his materials. As a dramatist he unerringly rejects whatever will destroy his dramatic purpose, correspondingly retaining every stroke which will tell. But his conservatism lies in his retaining, by reason of a certain faithfulness characteristic of him, many details in the old stories from which he derives his plays, which neither tell for nor against the dramatic effect. Thus Shakespeare found a wager which we should consider as grossly *contra bonos mores* to-day in Boccaccio's *Decameron*, his source for *Cymbeline*, a wager which, in modern England, could never be enforced by law and which, upon this basis, it would be absurd to have drawn up as in the play, by legal covenants. But the law of this play, if it comes to that, is not even the law of Boccaccio's late medieval Italy; it is the law of the mythical realm of Cymbeline, King of Great Britain, when Augustus reigned in Rome; and argument as to Shakespeare's knowledge or ignorance of what the English practice of his day may have been — to say nothing of contemporary law in Massachusetts — is preposterously irrelevant.

It has been said that the history of Shakespearean criticism consists largely in one triumph after another of the poet over the ignorance of his commentators. Take for example Queen Katherine's words to Cardinal Wolsey in *Henry VIII:*

> I do believe,
> Induced by potent circumstances, that
> You are mine enemy, and make my challenge.
> You shall not be my judge.

A Mr. Devecmon of the Maryland bar, we are informed, objects to this because, under our common law practice, it is the juror alone, and not the judge, who is subject to challenge. But in the Variorum *Merchant of Venice* will be found an interesting passage from a letter addressed to the late famous actor, Lawrence Barrett, in which we learn that Spanish law permits the challenge of a proposed juris-consult — or "master" as we might designate him — "for consanguinity, affinity or favor." And be it remembered that Katharine was of Spanish birth. We cannot affirm Shakespeare's knowledge or ignorance of a nice point such as this; but the recurrence of many such as to the law and other topics, creates a presumption that Shakespeare was accurate where accuracy seemed imperative, and careless of matters indifferent to the subject in hand.

But clearly there are many legal references in Shakespeare which are not referable merely to his sources and are only properly to be understood by a happy combination of legal learning with antiquarian lore. Sir George Greenwood contributes to our knowledge with just this happy combination in his justification of Shakespeare's use of the term "single bond" where Shylock says:

> Go with me to a notary, seal me there
> Your single bond.

"Bonds have usually a condition annexed to them that on the person bound paying so much money, or doing some specified act, the bond shall be void. A bond without a condition is called a single bond." [4] It would seem then, at first blush, that Shylock's bond was not a single bond, but one in which Antonio was bound on failure to pay to suffer the loss of a pound of flesh to Shylock. Sir George's explanation, however, is that this is not a condition "upon the performance of which the bond was to become void," but a penalty

---

[4] *Encyclopedia of the Laws of England*, ed. 1906, ii, 374.

attached, if he failed to pay.[5] So, too, in the matter of
the King's guardianship in *All's Well That Ends Well*.
It will be remembered that in consequence of her cure
of the King's illness, Helena, the daughter of a celebrated physician recently deceased, is granted the privilege of choosing whom she will for a husband. She
chooses the young count of Rousillon by whose mother
she had been reared and whom she had long secretly
loved; but the young scapegrace objects to a match on
the basis of such an inequality in rank. Whereupon
the king replies:

> 'Tis only title thou disdain'st in her, *the which*
> *I can build up.* . . . . .
> If thou canst like this creature as a maid,
> *I can create the rest:* virtue and she
> Is her own dower: *honor* and wealth from me.
> . . . Take her by the hand,
> And tell her she is thine: *to whom I promise*
> *A counterpoise: if not to thy estate,*
> *A balance more replete.*

Here on authority of the dictum of *Coke on Littleton*
that " the lord could not disparage the ward by a mes-
alliance," this passage has been pronounced " bad
law "; but the above words carefully read make clear
the power of the King, as the fountain of honor, " so to
ennoble ' the spouse ' as to make Helena ' of equal rank
with his ward.' " Sir George's interesting commentary
on a passage in *The Merry Wives of Windsor* in which
occur the technical words: *warrant, witness, waste,
fee simple, fine* and *recovery* will repay careful perusal,

---

[5] *Shakespeare's Law,* 25.

showing as it does a nice acquaintance with these technicalities as in use in Shakespeare's day, howsoever they are placed somewhat inappropriately in the mouth of Mistress Page, one of the merry wives of Windsor.

It would be tempting here to comment somewhat on the quibbles of Portia in the famous trial scene, on the absolute correctness of the proceedings as they are presented, in accordance with Latin, not English conditions; and I should like to follow the learned counsel in his able exposition of Elizabethan law in *Measure for Measure* as to the taking of a woman for a wife *per verba de praesenti*, this constituting a legal marriage. This explains the difficulties of the situation of not only Claudio and Juliet but of Angelo and Mariana as well in that most serious if forbidding play. But the general subject deserves presentation in an aspect somewhat wider before we leave it.

It is not the lawyers alone who have been impressed with the technical knowledge of Shakespeare. Physicians, alienists, naturalists, the student of history, the lover of the chase, even pedagogues, often find themselves amazed at the quality of Shakespeare's specific knowledge in matters of detail. And the reason is not so far to seek. In Bagehot's illuminating phrase, "Shakespeare's was an experiencing genius." What to the lawyer, the doctor, the naturalist is a matter painfully acquired by specific study, is to the playwright's intuitive genius the flash of a moment. It is this in which Shakespeare's greatness, his comprehensiveness, largely subsists. I never weary of repeating that there is absolutely nothing mysterious about Shakespeare except his genius, and this I repeat because it is so necessary that we remember it. The inference that Shakespeare must have studied law because he has *fines* and *recoveries* down pat, is just as rational as that which makes him a falconer because *tiercel gentle, jesses, haggard, eyas,* and the rest of the technical words of hawking are always correctly employed by him. He has been made a schoolmaster because Page's son in *The Merry Wives* can correctly decline *hic, haec, hoc:* though even this will not make him a Latinist.

With every respect for the learning and argumentative acumen of Sir George in this and other works, I submit, as the lawyers say, that we cannot wrest the secret of Shakespeare's greatness by means of an investigation into his expert or inexpert knowledge of any technical art. This is the raiment he wears, not the man within; and his masks were many, howsoever the essential man beneath remains ever the same in his unmatchable grasp of those larger things which cannot be weighed in scales and adjudicated on the bases of precedent.

Has it ever occurred to some of our distinguished members of the bar that history, science and philosophy would be impossible were their processes confined to the processes of the law; were their proofs dependent on the limitations set for legal evidences? The existence and foundation of courts of equity go to prove this repugnance in human nature to the rigidities of conventional legal process; there must be an appeal to something wider than mere precedent. It is somewhat to be expected, then, that we should find a large proportion of those who are visited by "historic doubts" as to Shakespeare and others, who are. troubled about "problems" where no actual problems exist, should be lawyers or men of legal cast of mind. To men thus highly and specifically trained the weighing of evidence is a far more interesting process than the exercise of the historic imagination; to such, trivialities bulk large and obscure realities; and thus they come often to theorize about matters the determination of which is utterly unimportant to gods and to men.

I wonder if Shakespeare was always so clever in these small things as some of us think. It is affirmed that he knows all about a horse, and the chase, and falconry and the popular names and habits of birds, insects and flowers: how could he help all this, country-bred lad that he was? Of sports, too, he was a master. As to human passions, conduct, character, deportment — humanity was his subject matter; it was his daily vocation to study mankind: and we must grant him an observer. Even in this matter of the law, Shakespeare's father was litigious and his father's son after him, as the discoveries of more lawsuits in which he was more or less concerned, have gone of late further to prove.[6] A clever young man can learn almost as much in personal contact with the courts as a duller youth in a law school. The difference between a specialist and a genius lies largely in the fact that the spe-

[6] The various unearthings of W. C. Wallace.

cialist is usually burdened with his learning; the genius, with twice as much, still treads lightly armed and at ease. Until we cease applying the petty technical standards of our own littleness to the stature of greatness, we shall not understand men like Shakespeare. It is better to read him than all these clever brochures about what he knew or did not know, what he was or who he was not, and this extends to comments like this of mine on their cleverness. If the personal opinion of one who is not sure whether he is a lawyer or not is of any moment in a case such as this, I should say that Shakespeare's knowledge of the law, like his knowledge of everything else, was that of a man who saw life directly, not life refracted through books; it was accurate to an amazing degree where he had occasion to fix his gaze; careless, where carelessness affected no damage to his art, and generally far above that ordinary level of information which we demand and get of other men. The accumulation of every scrap in his works that has to do with the law, technically or otherwise, and the weighing of it all with reference to his age, his sources, the lore back of it, and the rest, would be a delightful piece of work, especially for the legal mind, but it would bring us no nearer a verdict. To speak in the mode of lawyers, there is much in life, in art and in criticism that must ever remain in a state, *pendente lite*.

IX

DEVOTIONAL POETRY IN THE REIGN OF CHARLES I

SINCE THE DAYS of the venerable Bede and his beautiful story of the divine call to a poetic mission given to Caedmon, English poets have paid their tithe and more to the celebration of religious subjects, whether in translation, paraphrase, or in the expression of their own religious emotions. By the unerring instinct that makes the artist of one age the kin of all artists to come, poets have been especially attracted to that union of genuine devotion with the highest form of lyrical expression, the *Psalms of David*.[1] If we leave paraphrase, which extended to nearly all the noble stories of the *Old Testament* and to many of the *New,* reaching its climax in the divine cosmogony of *Paradise Lost,* we shall find this religious spirit often communicated, even in otherwise original poetry, in the very terms of Biblical style and phrase; but, despite this, preserving in the product a tone and sanction above mediocrity of thought or unoriginality of diction. " It would not be easy to find a sonnet in any

---

[1] Wyatt, Surrey, Sternhold and Hopkins, and Parker, all had paraphrased some of the *Psalms* before Elizabeth's accession; Gascoigne, Sidney and Bacon — to mention only chief names — in her reign; Milton, Bishop King and Sandys later.

language," says Mark Pattison, " of equal power to vibrate through all the fibres of feeling with Sonnet XIX, *Avenge, O Lord, thy slaughtered innocents.* The new and nobler purpose to which Milton puts the sonnet is here in its splendor: ' In his hand the thing became a trumpet whence he blew soul-animating strains.' Yet with what homely material is the effect produced: not only is there not a single purple patch in the wording, but of thought, or image, all that there is is a borrowed thought, and one repeatedly borrowed, *viz.,* Tertullian's saying, ' the blood of the martyrs is the seed of the Church.' It would not be impossible, but it would be sacrilege to point to distinct faults in this famous piece; yet we may say that with a familiar quotation for its only thought and with diction almost below the ordinary, its thoughtful flood of suppressed passion sweeps along the hackneyed Biblical phrases of which it is composed, just as a swollen river rolls before it the worn pebbles long ago brought down from the mountain-side. From this sonnet we may learn that the poetry of a poem is lodged somewhere else than in its matter or its thoughts, or its imagery, or its words. Our heart is here taken by storm, but not by any of those things. The poet hath breathed on us, and we have received his inspiration. In this sonnet is realized Wordsworth's definition of poetry: ' the spontaneous overflow of powerful feeling.' " [2]

We have here the secret of the greater diversity of opinion which exists in critical estimates of certain

[2] *The Sonnets of Milton,* 58.

"divine poets" as compared with our current estimates of their profaner brethren. It is not granted to everyone to be at all times in the mood in which the sincerity of the devotional poet can awaken a responsive chord. The greatest of poets can compel this response most generally, and therein lies much of their power; those less great often fail, not so much because of their own defects, as because the music which they offer falls upon deaf ears, or ears deadened and ringing with the din of things wherein is neither poetry nor life.

It might be hard to find two devotional poets whose artistic ideals were more widely at variance with those of today than Francis Quarles and George Wither. Even their ethical purpose, though worthy of all praise as an ethical purpose, was proceeded about in a manner so foreign to our manner in such matters, that it is difficult for us fairly to appreciate their achievement. Yet to have given solace and moral support to thousands of their fellow countrymen — for these men were read and re-read, Quarles in innumerable editions, like Tupper in the days of our fathers — to have given this solace with that modicum of literary buoyancy which was sufficient to float the moralizing, the didacticism and other heavy matters in the somewhat dense medium for which it was intended, is surely no trifle. The flippancy of thought into which a figure may betray one cannot diminish the historical importance of such writers, although it may well remain a question how far the application of poetry of any species to specific needs and occasions may take it out of the category of the fine arts.

If the reader will consider the practice of devotional poetry in the sixteenth century as contrasted with the practice of it in the age under consideration, he will discover several points of interest. If we except such an enthusiastic devotee as Father Southwell, few poets of the earlier age were as undividedly devotional in their themes as were Quarles, Herbert, Sandys, Crashaw and Vaughan. Nor is this unexplainable; the earlier age had been much taken up with the world and its beauties; the new age, with the world and its vanities. It was no part of Anglican Catholicism to quarrel with what was beautiful in the world; it was regarded in the spirit of worship to use and enjoy what has been granted us for use and enjoyment. Far different is it in an age in which the deep self-questionings of Puritanism had discovered, or thought to have discovered, nothing but deception, vanity and idleness in the shows of the world. The cleavage between the aesthetic and the ethical view of the purpose of literature is complete, and the poets no longer write, as did Spenser, hymns to earthly and to heavenly love and beauty, bound lovingly together in one volume; but devote themselves solely to the celebration of one or the other, as did Carew and Herbert, or poignantly regret the earthly leanings of their earlier Muses as did Wither and Vaughan.

The earlier poets too seemed at times to write devotional verse as a sort of duty, like going to church, the proper thing to do. This continued, and we feel that Herrick — poor pagan that he was — hardly wrote some of his prayers to God, with the same naturalness and abandon with which he addressed Juno, Venus or Apollo. The latter was a matter to sport with and no danger; on the best authority there were no such personages as these statuesque delightful old pagan gods — would that there were! The former was a very different affair; like the wearing of Sunday clothes, a serious matter, and not to be done lightly or altogether comfortably, except for a sustaining sense of decorum. Greatly in contrast is the beautiful and spiritually devoted feeling of Herbert, a man who humbly and devoutly held his poetical gift in trust that he might therewith do the will of God. Isaak Walton's touching account of Herbert's delivery of the manuscript of his book of poetry, *The Temple,* almost upon his deathbed, cannot be too often quoted: " He did, with so sweet a humility as seemed to exalt him, bow down to Mr. Duncan, and with a thoughtful and contented look, say to him : ' Sir, O pray deliver this little book to my dear brother, Ferrar, and tell him he shall find in it a picture of the many spiritual conflicts that have passed twixt God and my soul, before I could subject mine to the will of Jesus, my Master, in whose service I have now found perfect freedom; desire him to read it, and then, if he can think it may turn to the advantage of any dejected poor soul, let it be made public; if not, let him burn it, for I and it are the least of God's mercies.' " [3]

Notwithstanding the richness and variety of the religious and moral poetry that dignifies the age of Elizabeth, the devotional poetry of the Caroline period

[3] Walton's *Lives,* ed. Morley, 277.

has gained in fervor and depth of thought. We cannot say that it retained that finish and sense of artistic design which continued longer to pervade secular poetry. The devotional poet has his eye almost wholly upon the subject, and the very spontaneity of his emotions hurries him on — if he be less than the greatest — to the facile verbosity of Wither, the metrical lapses of Quarles, or the ruggedness and defective execution of Vaughan. In a man like Milton the artistic instinct on the other hand is so strong that sincerity of workmanship becomes a feature of his very worship. To praise God with less than the perfection of man's power is impiety; and even the fervor of passion must ever be the controlling regulation of human activity. Thus it is that in the self-contained and at times to us somewhat cold and austere Miltonic poetry, we have really a higher form of worship in art than we get from didactic Wither, saintlike Herbert, or rapturous Crashaw. In Milton we have the adoration of a great and sincere soul, a man who had known the chastening of adversity, a man who had sacrificed all, and indeed lost much, that he might do the duty nearest him.

Let us consider now somewhat these products of the devotional poets of the reign of Charles. Quarles and Wither both began writing in the reign of James. If we except the several devotional verse-pamphlets of Nicholas Breton and some others of earlier times, Quarles was one of the first and long remained by far the most popular of what may be termed the devotional pamphleteers. As early as 1621 he had published his *Hadessa, the History of Queen Esther,* followed by *Sion's Elegies,* 1624, and several other books of devotional verse. Many of these, as their titles indicate, are paraphrases of Biblical story, but in *Sion's Elegies* and *Sion's Sonnets* we have the devotional lyric. The idea of a collection of such poems in a sort of continuance Quarles probably derived from Wither's *Hymns and Songs of the Church,* 1623; sequences of "divine sonnets," as they were called, had been well known among the writings of men like Constable and Breton before the close of the last century. Wither's book "comprehends the canonical hymns, and such parcels of Holy Scripture as may properly be sung, with some other ancient songs . . . appropriated to the several tunes and occasions observable in the church of England." There is a hymn in the companion volume, *Haleluiah,* 1641, "When oppressors and wicked men flourish," for one "legally censured, whether justly or unjustly," "for one that is promoted," "a thanksgiving after drought."[4] The fatherly solicitude of this worthy versifier provided for every sort and condition of man and for every contingency of life. The poet of *Fair Virtue,* Wither's delightful volume of secular verse, has almost disappeared, except for a certain naïveté and fluency in verse which marks everything that this facile writer touched. All ornament, figure and epithet has been ruthlessly destroyed until the verse is as direct and unadorned as the baldest prose and scarcely more in-

---

[4] Reprinted by the Spenser Society. There is some entertaining reading on the function of sacred poetry in the preface to this volume.

spired. The following is a fair specimen of this devotional commonplace:

> O hear us though we still offend,
> Augment our wasted store;
> Into this land that plenty send
> Which filled it heretofore;
> Then give us grace to use it so
> That thou may'st pleaséd be,
> And that when fuller we shall grow
> We think not less on thee.[5]

In most respects no two poets could present more opposite methods than Wither and Quarles. There may be some figures of speech in the devotional verse of Wither, I have not found them; Quarles is nothing if not abundantly and grotesquely figurative, allegorical, and enigmatic. Wither is direct in construction if garrulous and of easy flapping onward flight; Quarles is at times much twisted and contorted, and soars after his kind with absurd intermittent flops and downfalls. Quarles too is garrulous; but while Wither is apt to say the same thing about many things, Quarles says a great many things about the same thing.

The most famous book of Quarles is his *Emblems,* 1635. This was altogether the most popular book of verse published during the century. It is still reprinted for religious edification with a reproduction of the hideous, allegorical wood-cuts of the original edition. Although his verse is much overgrown with conceits, repetition and verbiage, and impaired by slovenly versification (a fault which Quarles shares

[5] *Haleluiah,* ed. Spenser Soc. 129.

with contemporaries far greater than he), there is much real poetry in Quarles. In moments of fervid religious excitement the gauds and baubles of Quarles' ordinary poetic diction drop away and he writes with manly directness:

> O whither shall I fly? what path untrod
> Shall I seek out to scape the flaming rod
> Of my offended, of my angry God?
>
> Where shall I sojourn? what kind sea will hide
> My head from thunder? where shall I abide,
> Until his flames be quenched or laid aside?
>
> What if my feet should take their hasty flight,
> And seek protection in the shades of night?
> Alas, no shades can blind the God of Light.[6]

Two years earlier Herbert's *Temple* had appeared and at once had taken a hold upon the hearts of readers. George Herbert was a gentleman and a scholar. He had been orator of his university, courtier and a man of the world. Like Quarles, in his coarser manner, Herbert reached the serious readers of his age with his sincerity, his piety, his rhetorical if somewhat artificial and " conceited " style and his originality of figure. He went much further, for Herbert, whatever be his rank amongst others, is a true poet who, alike in form and spirit, often raises the particular idea into the sphere of the universal and makes it a thing of new beauty and potency.

Passing the devotional part of William Habington's

[6] *Emblems,* ed. 1823, p. 124.

Castara, 1639–40, a somewhat tedious professional gentleman whose work is as bookish and imitative as himself, we reach the scriptural paraphrases of George Sandys, the traveller, including a complete and excellent version of the *Psalms, Job,* and *Ecclesiastes.* The dignified original poem *Deo Optimo Maximo* is a good specimen of the devotional eloquence of Sandys, who appears to have been a man of fine fibre and delicacy of feeling. Sandys was among Caroline devotional poets what Waller was among the amorists and writers of occasional verse, a man whose somewhat formal and restrained nature lent itself readily to the reaction in rhetoric and versification which was setting in. This is the more notable from the fact that Sandys alone of the class of writers to which he belongs, was treated with respect by the critics of the age to come, and allowed a rank correspondent to his historical position.

In 1646 appeared *Steps to the Temple,* with a few secular poems under the sub-title, *The Delights of the Muses,* by Richard Crashaw. The *Steps* were so named in modest reference and relation to Herbert's *Temple,* which is Crashaw's immediate inspiration. Crashaw, while a student at Cambridge, came under influences which, considering the difference in the two ages are not incomparable to the Oxford or Tractarian Movement of the century of Newman. In the fervent and pious life of Nicholas Ferrar, into whose hands we have already seen the dying Herbert confiding his poetry, Crashaw found much to emulate and admire. Ferrar, notable in science and a successful man of affairs, forsook the world and formed, with his kinfolk about him, a little religious community at Little Giddings in Huntingdonshire, where he sought to lead a spiritual life in accord with the principles of the Anglican Church. The artistic temperament of Crashaw had led him early " to denounce those who disassociate art from religious worship "; the charity and benignity of his temper caused him equally to oppose those who made an attack upon the papacy an article of faith. It is easy to see how this attitude, under spiritual influences of men such as Herbert and Ferrar should gradually have led Crashaw, with the help of some added political impetus, over to the old faith. The picture of Cowley, the loyal, fair-minded, meditative Epicurean, befriending Crashaw, the young enthusiast, when the latter was deprived of his fellowship and both were exiled in a foreign country, is pleasant to dwell upon. For Cowley was comparatively fortunate among the exiles as secretary to the queen of Charles. Crashaw must have been almost in want. It was the influence of Cowley that procured for Crashaw, now a priest in the Roman Church, a post in the service of Cardinal Palotta. But it was not for long. Crashaw died in the year of the execution of King Charles, a sub-canon in the church at Loretto.

The relation of Crashaw to Herbert, save for his discipleship, which changed very little Crashaw's distinctive traits, is much that of Herrick and Carew. Herbert and Crashaw were both good scholars; Herbert knew the world and put it aside as vanity; Crashaw could never have been of the world, his was a nature alien to it; and yet there is a greater warmth in Crashaw than in Herbert. Crashaw turns the passions of earth to worship and identifies the spiritual and the material in his devotion; Herbert with all his love of ritual, has somewhat of the Puritan spirit in him, which is troubled in the contemplation of earthly vanities and struggles to rise above and beyond them. It is the antithesis of Protestantism and Roman Catholicism, an antithesis which we can understand better if we can bring ourselves to sympathize with each, than if we seek to throw ourselves into an attitude of attack or defense of either.

In matter of poetic style too, despite his quips and conceits, and the fact that with him, as with many devotional poets, execution sometimes waits upon the thought and comes halting after, Herbert is far more self-constrained and his poetry of more uniform workmanship and excellence. But if Herbert has never fallen into Crashaw's extravagances, he is equally incapable of his inspired, rhapsodic flights. Herbert felt the beauties of this visible world and has some delicate touches of appreciation, as where he says:

> I wish I were a tree
> For sure then I should grow
> To fruit or shade; at least some bird would trust
> Her household to me, and I should be just.

Crashaw knows less of the concrete objects of the world, but is a creature of light and atmosphere, and revels in color and the gorgeousness thereof. Crashaw

often rhapsodizes without bridle, and is open at times
to grave criticism on the score of taste. It is for these
shortcomings that he has been, time out of mind, the
stock example of the dreadful things into which the ill
regulated poetical fancy may fall. The " sister baths "
and " portable oceans " of *Magdalene* are easily ridiculed; but it is almost as easy, while ridiculing these
distortions of fancy, to forget the luminousness and
radiance, the uncommon imaginative power and vola-
tility of mind of this devout Shelley of the reign of
Charles I.[7]

Two years after the first edition of Crashaw's poems
appeared Herrick's *Noble Numbers,* bearing date
1647, but bound in after the *Hesperides,* 1648. Herrick was too good a poet not to write well on any
theme, and some of these devotional and moral poems
have the same naïve and dainty charm that is possessed in fuller measure by their more worldly sisters.
The stately and gracious forms of Anglican worship
must have been dear to such a man as Herrick; but it
is unlikely that any deep spiritual yearnings disturbed
the peaceful serenity of Dean's Prior. Herrick is best
when his devotional poetry touches the picturesque
details of his own life in poems like *The Grange, A
Thanksgiving for His House,* or when the subject
grows out of a touching Biblical situation which may
be elaborated with art, as in the fine *Dirge for Jeph-
thah's Daughter.*[8] But even these sincere and beautiful religious lyrics are as ripples on a shallow lake

[7] *Herbert,* ed. Grosart, 40.
[8] *Herrick,* ed. Hale, 109, 143, 147.

to the crested waves of Crashaw or the deep sea stir-
rings of Vaughan.

If we look forward we shall find the practice of the
sustained religious narrative poem, first popularized
by Quarles, continuing down to very late times. Thus
Cowley wrote an epic the *Davideis;* and Prior esteemed
his *Solomon* the best of his work. Parnell wrote on
Moses, Deborah, Hezekiah and others, Blackmore on
all *Creation;* whilst the seemly and graceful turning
out of a hymn, meditation or short Biblical paraphrase
became one of the ordinary accomplishments of a gentleman. No less a celebrity than the eminent Mr.
Waller wrote two short cantos *Of Divine Poesy* with
poetical reflections on the Lord's Prayer; and his great
successors, Dryden and Pope, did not disdain to follow his example in the decorous, if occasional, practice of a like art.

The gracious and musical lyrics of Andrew Marvell
were written in all probability before he took service
under the Commonwealth in 1652. Like Milton,
Marvell laid aside the companionship of the Muses to
fight worldly battles for what he believed to be the
right; but, unlike Milton, he never returned to poetry
again, but remained in the toil and sweat of battle to
the last. Marvell's devotional poems are only a few,
but there is about them, as about all the lyrical verse
which this rare poet has left us, a moral wholesome-
ness, a genuine joy in external nature, and withal so
well contained a grace of expression that Marvell must
be assigned no mean place among the lyrists of his
century. Curiously enough Marvell has extended the

pastoral to embrace religious poetry in one or two not unsuccessful efforts. The ode celebrating the nativity, which from its theme always partook of the pastoral nature, was to be sure no new thing; and Herrick, with others before him, had applied the pastoral to occasional verse.[9] Marvell's poems are different, and while didactic in intent are yet distinctly artistic. Such poems are *Clorinda and Damon* and *A Dialogue between Thyrsis and Dorinda.*[10]

There remains one great name, that of Henry Vaughan, the Silurist, whose secular verse, published as early as 1646, was succeeded by long years of religious study and contemplation, and the production of many books in verse and prose, all devotional in cast. Vaughan knew Randolph and Cartwright and venerated the memory of Jonson, who died when Vaughan was a youth at Oxford; under his influence he translated Juvenal and wrote some erotic poetry not above that of Randolph or Stanley. From the little we knew of his life, it seems that Vaughan, like Herbert, had been of the world in his younger days, and that the chastening hand of adversity had fallen heavily upon him and led him away from earthly themes to the contemplative and devout life of a recluse. Without violence to the probable facts, we may conceive of Vaughan in his beautiful home in South Wales, as we think of Wordsworth in later times, in his beloved Lake Country, a lover of woods and hills and

[9] Cf." A Pastoral upon the Birth of Prince Charles," *ibid.,* 35.
[10] *Marvell,* ed. Aitken, 41, 77.

the life that makes them melodious; but a lover of them not merely for their beauty, but for the divine message which they bear to man, their revelation and ethical import. Vaughan's nature like that of Wordsworth is at once expansive and narrow. This expansiveness of the two poets indeed is not unlike; and rests upon a large-souled interpretation of the goodness of God as revealed to man in his works; in a loving appreciation and tenderness for nature, in a revealing ethical insight and in a " high seriousness " intent on worthy themes. On the other hand both poets were narrow, though differing in their limitations. To Wordsworth, doubts, fears and the complexities of modern life were naught; they did not exist for him. Vaughan had put the world from him, although he had known it; and still heard it from afar, like the hum of a great and wicked city, out of which his soul had been delivered. Wordsworth, with all his greatness, was narrowed by egotism, by didacticism, by pride; Vaughan, far less — if at all — by any of these, than by his theology; which is often hard and formal, and at times unlovely. Vaughan was also limited at times by an imperfect artistic sense and a halting execution.

Vaughan's " realism in detail " which is based not only upon a close observance of nature but upon a sympathy and love extending to all created creatures, seems a heritage from a nobler age. In no one of his immediate contemporaries do we find it in the same strength and imbued with the same tenderness; not in the grand descriptive eloquence of Milton, in the homeliness of Marvel, nor in the sensuous delight of Herrick. It is thus that Vaughan addresses a bird:

Hither thou com'st. The busy wind all night
Blew through thy lodging, where thy own warm wing
Thy pillow was. Many a sullen storm,
For which coarse man seems much the fitter born,
  Rained in thy bed
  And harmless head;
And now as fresh and cheerful as the light
Thy little heart in early hymns doth sing
Unto that Providence, whose unseen arm
Curbed them, and clothed thee well and warm.[11]

In Vaughan's mysticism we have a more general trait of the religious poet, a trait not more peculiar in this age to Vaughan than to Crashaw. Mysticism of symbol, whether it manifest itself in poetry or in philosophy and religion, is one of the most difficult subjects with which the critic has to deal, for it demands a sympathetic power to assume the momentary subjective position of the author at once with a complete reconstruction of his mood. The religious mysticism of Vaughan is distinguishable from that of Crashaw, chiefly in the fact that Vaughan is less ecstatic and more musingly meditative; less purely emotional, although, when roused, stirred to the inner deeps of his nature. Not the least interesting quality of the poetry of Vaughan is its intellectuality, a quality which we are apt to think opposed to the spontaneity of emotion which inspires the highest forms of art and that natu-

[11] "The Bird," *Sacred Poems of Vaughan*, ed, Lyte, 174.

ralness or inevitability of expression, in which the highest art is ever clothed. Yet intellectuality is alike the glory of Donne and of Robert Browning. It is not that art is to be regarded as a production into which the rational processes enter very little as compared with the emotions; but rather that such a proportion of the impelling emotion and the regulative reason be preserved as neither to degrade the product into mere sensuousness, nor to change its nature from art, which is the presentation of the typified image, to philosophy, which is the rational distinction of its actual properties. A wanton confusion of images which neither reveal and figure forth, nor distinguish and make clear, is neither art nor philosophy, but a base product that fails utterly of the purposes of either.

We have thus traversed a period of scarcely sixty years and found in it a body of devotional poetry of a quantity and a quality for which we may look in vain in any other half century of English literature. A superficial consideration of this century is apt to divide all England into the hostile camps of Roundhead and Cavalier; to consider all the former hypocrites, and all the latter good loyal men; or — as is more usual in America — to assume all supporters of kings utterly misguided; whilst in the Puritan and other rebels alone can we believe that the virtues could ever have flourished. In the face of these vulgar prejudices, it is interesting to note that among the devotional poets of the reign of Charles and later, Habington and Crashaw were Romanists; Wither, Milton, Marvell (though " no Roundhead " as his most recent editor puts it) were Puritans, and all the others were members of the established church. The spirit of devotion which sought utterance in verse rose superior to the narrowness of mere dogma and the inspiration of poetry waited not alone on a favored sect. Indeed nothing could better prove the strong religious feeling which continued to animate the average Englishman of the seventeenth century than the great popularity of books like Quarles' and Herbert's among the communicants of the Church of England. The Non-Conformists had their imaginative literature too, and produced in this century a man who, if not a poet, is almost everything else that literature can demand. *Pilgrim's Progress* is not much later than the latest work of Vaughan and marks a long step forward when compared to the contorted and mystical allegory of Quarles. In devotional literature, as in secular, the coming age was the age of prose, and in this immortal work the change was already complete.

With the return of Charles and the exiles, the popularity of religious verse decreased, controversial prose coming more and more to take its place with devout readers. However some few lesser poets of conservative tastes, like John Norris of Bemerton, continued to cultivate "divine poetry" far into the last quarter of the century. *Samson Agonistes* and the great epics of Milton do not concern us directly here, although they are the loftiest poetical utterances which the English Muse has devoted to religion. It is well known that contemporary influences contributed little to them, and that they were written upon a long-formed determination, and come as the late and crowning glory of a rich poetical past. The poems of Milton have lost somewhat in our day of rational thinking; criticism shudders at a cosmogony in which Christian legend and pagan mythology are mingled in Titanic confusion. It is with *Paradise Lost* much as it is with the stately fugues of John Sebastian Bach, the father of modern music. We prefer something very different. Let us not offend such poetic and musical taste as may be left us by allusion to qualities which the vogue of the moment governs. But the undergrowth of the arts, with its weeds or brambles, has existed in every age to live its day and fade with the evanescent flowerings that wither as the seasons wane and change. It is the tall trees that last, renewed in fresh beauty age after age, and it is the larger arts that endure beyond the moment of their creation to give new joy and consolation to those who come to know them.

X

THE SUPERNATURAL IN OLD ENGLISH DRAMA

THE ELIZABETHAN attitude towards the world that lies beyond, push forward the barriers of human knowledge as we may, was very different from our own. Before what Arthur Hugh Clough wittily called "the Supreme Bifurcation," the Elizabethan never paused in modern puzzled, agnostic doubt, but confidently chose his horn of the dilemma and cheerfully suffered his tossing or goring as the case might be. Astrologers, alchemists, and wisewomen flourished and grew rich on the ignorance and credulity of their dupes; tellers of fortunes, mixers of philters, finders of hidden treasure and lost articles by divination prospered alike. Many, like Owen Glendower, could "call spirits from the vasty deep," and "command the devil; " and few there were, like Hotspur, to question, "Will they come when you do call for them? " Nor were these superstitions confined to the ignorant and the vulgar. The Earl of Leicester consulted the celebrated astrologer Doctor Dee as to the auspicious day on which to hold the coronation of of Queen Elizabeth. Excellent Reginald Scot, although he humanely wrote a very long book to display the shallowness of the evidence on which witches were convicted, did not venture to deny the existence of witchcraft;[1] and even Bacon, who incredulously doubted the Copernican system of astronomy, shared with his royal master King James a belief in many of the popular superstitions of his day.[2] In an environment such as this, the supernatural as a dramatic motive had a sanction and a potency well nigh inconceivable today.

The supernatural first entered English drama as an artistic motive with the advent of *Faustus*. "Of all that [Marlowe] hath written for the stage," wrote Edward Philips, "his *Doctor Faustus* hath made the greatest noise."[3] And many editions and alterations for revival point to this as having been one of the most popular dramas of the day. As we have it *The Tragical History of Doctor Faustus* is little more than a succession of scenes void of continuity or cohesion, except for the unity of the main figure and the unrelenting progress of the whole towards the overwhelming catastrophe. Moreover, this fragment is disfigured and disgraced by the interpolation of scenes of clownage and ribaldry which, in view of the strictures enunciated in the famous prologue of *Tamburlaine* as to "such conceits as clownage keeps in pay," and the apology of the printer in the preface of that play, it is next to impossible to believe that Marlowe wrote. And yet, broken torso that it is, there is a grandeur

---

[1] *The Discoverie of Witchcraft*, 1584.
[2] See *Sylva Sylvarum, passim.*
[3] *Theatrum Poetarum* (1675), ed. 1800, 113.

beyond mere description in this conception of the lonely, grace-abandoned scholar, in whom the promptings of remorse alone betray the touch of human weakness, whose inordinate desire for power and knowledge, rather than mere gratification of appetite, have impelled to the signing of his terrible compact with the Evil One, and whose mortal agonies have in them a dignity which not even the mediaeval conception of hoofed and horned deviltry could destroy. Perilous is the practice of the art of comparison, and yet, when all has been said, there remains an impassioned reserve, a sense of mastery and a poignancy of feeling about this battered fragment of the old Elizabethan age that I find not in the grotesque Teutonic *diablerie*, the symbolical aesthetics, even in the consummate poetic art, wisdom, and philosophy of Goethe's *Faust*.

The story of Faustus, with its conjuring of demons, its infernal compact, the alternate promptings of the good and bad angel, and its appalling catastrophe, is a mediaeval story of black art. There seems little reason to doubt that the " white magic " of the English Friar Bacon was worked into his romantic drama, *Friar Bacon and Friar Bungay,* by Robert Greene in direct emulation of the foreign black magic of Marlowe's *Faustus.* The romantic part of Greene's engaging play tells of the love of Prince Edward for the Fair Maid of Fressingfield, a keeper's daughter, with the fair maid's anticipation of the rôle of Priscilla, in *The Courtship of Miles Standish,* in favor of her lover Lacey, Earl of Lincoln. But with this is united a tale of the magical doings of Friar Bacon — how he created by his art a brazen head that spoke and would have walled all England with brass, but for the stupidity of a servant, how he could show the acts of people afar off in his "prospective stone" of crystal, and obliterate both time and space—for such was the myth which had grown out of the life and reputed studies of that remarkable man, Roger Bacon.

The story of Faustus revolves about the daring compact with the father of evil and its terrible fruit; the characters, save for the writhing and tortured protagonist and the supernatural ministers to his ambition and his fate, seem thin and unreal, as the daylight seems unreal after a night of fever and anguish. Friar Bacon, on the contrary, is a goodnatured and patriotic wizard, solicitous for the happiness and the good of others, alive in fresh and merry England; and although the shadow of his intercourse with hell hangs over him, a misadventure, for which his art is only indirectly responsible, brings him to repentance and the renouncement of his traffic with evil. A novel feature of the story (in the original tale as in the play) is the necromantic contest in which Friar Bacon worsts Vandermast, a rival magician, and has him transported to his native Germany on the back of a simulacrum of Hercules.[4] It was this feature of the contest that Anthony Munday imitated in his *John a Kent and John a Cumber,* 1594,[5] a diverting comedy of situation in which the two wizards who give title to the play are pitted against each other in an elaborate exhibition of

---

[4] *Friar Bacon and Friar Bungay,* Scene ix.
[5] *Publications of the Shakespeare Society,* 1851.

their supernatural powers, in process of which disguises, exchanges of person, "errors," and "antiques" figure in bewildering confusion. Munday's play is doubtless original, although his heroine, Sedanen, was known to the popular ballads of the day, and John a Kent appears to have been an actual person living near Hereford at some remote and indeterminable period, and enjoying the reputation of having sold himself to the devil, like Faustus.

The infernal compact appears once more in the pleasing anonymous comedy of *The Merry Devil of Edmonton*, 1606; but Peter Fabel, the English Faustus, after exercising his art on the devil to cheat him into a seven years' prolongation of his time on earth,[6] like Bacon and John a Kent, employs his powers to unite faithful lovers, and the supernatural ceases to be an element in the story. A remarkable application of the infernal compact to an historical subject is *The Devil's Charter, or a Tragedy Containing the Life and Death of Pope Alexander VI*, acted by the king's company in 1606, the work of Barnaby Barnes, the lyrist, who is not otherwise known to the history of the drama.[7] Alexander's wicked and abandoned life and the marvelous success of his worldly career, crowned with the papacy, gave rise almost immediately upon his death to stories in which he was transmuted in the popular imagination into a species of pontifical Faustus. Nor did the Protestant zeal of succeeding times

[6] See the opening scene.

[7] This interesting play has been reprinted by R. B. McKerrow in *Materealien Zur Kunde*, 1904.

neglect an example at once so flagrant and so apt. Barnes's tragedy is full of horror and novel situation, and owes not a little to the study of Marlowe's *Faustus*. A fine and original climax is produced when the wicked Pope, about to die, drags himself from his couch that he may sit once more in the seat of St. Peter and feel the triple tiara on his brow. With faltering steps and eager, trembling hands, he approaches the curtain which veils the papal chair. He draws it and starts back, for there, arrayed in all the regalia of priestly pomp, crowned and occupying St. Peter's throne, sits Satan himself. Had Barnaby Barnes known when to stay his hand, and had he been somewhat more of a practical playwright, this tragedy might not have been an altogether unworthy successor of its illustrious prototype.

Closely allied to these dramas in which supernatural powers are derived by a magician from the pledging of his soul are the several plays which represent the devil in human guise and familiar intercourse with mortals, to their undoing, or satirically to the worsting of the devil. Henslowe records a production, the work of Day and Haughton, entitled *Friar Rush and the Proud Woman of Amsterdam*.[8] Friar Rush is well known in continental folklore as the devil disguised as a cook who corrupts a whole monastery with delicious fare. As a prose tale Friar Rush had already appeared in England as early as 1568. And although no known version contains allusion to the woman of Amsterdam, several of the friar's well known exploits may well

[8] *Henslowe's Diary*, ed. Greg, ii, 218.

have been transferred to the Flemish capital.[9] It was not until 1610 that Dekker produced his extraordinary stage elaboration of the story of Friar Rush, *If This Be Not a Good Play the Devil is in It*. This play represents the mission of three devils sent by the infernal council to earth, one of whom, Ruffman, practices on the virtuous court of Naples, a second, Lurchall, on a hitherto upright merchant, the third, Friar Rush, on a monastery renowned for the austerity of its rule. The demons succeed in bringing all save a steadfast sub-prior to the verge of ruin; and the play ends with a realistic representation of the tortures of the villainous merchant Bartervile, in company with such sensational contemporary malefactors as Ravaillac and Guy Fawkes. Dekker's play was hastily written and is confused in places in its design, and grotesque alike for the vulgar excess of its *diablerie* and for its transference to modern times of a story incongruous when deprived of its fitting mediaeval setting. And yet *If This Be Not a Good Play* cannot but be regarded as a very remarkable effort for the boldness of its plan, the comprehensiveness of its scope, and the surprising anticipation which it offers of Goethe's *Faust* in its "recasting of an old devil story in terms of modern society." [10]

Dekker's play has no relation whatever to Machiavelli's *jeu d'esprit* on the marriage of Belphegor, although a superficial resemblance was noted by Langbaine, and this suggestion has misled some later writ-

[9] Herford, *Literary Relations of England and Germany* (1886), 308.
[10] *Ibid.*, 317.

ers.[11] Machiavelli's *novella* is, however, the direct source of the main plot of *Grim the Collier of Croydon*, the printed title of which is derived from the under-plot in which an inferior demon disguised as Robin Goodfellow figures in a farcical rôle. The major plot of *Grim the Collier* details how a suicide, Spenser's Malbecco,[12] pleading before the infernal judges that he was driven in desperation to his crime by the outrageous wickedness of his wife, is reprieved for a year and a day, while the devil, Belphegor, is dispatched to earth to observe if womankind is really so desperately depraved as reported.[13] Belphegor plans to marry one woman, and is duped into marriage with another. Both men and women prove to be more than a match in ingenuity and wickedness for the unhappy devil; and in the end, buffeted and outwitted, poisoned by his wife, and waylaid by her paramour, he is only saved from the gallows on a false accusation of murder by the timely expiration of his term on earth. St. Dunstan appears in this play, as in one or two others, as from his wisdom and sanctity a controller of evil; but he never rises to the dignity of a magician.[14]

In the year of Shakespeare's death, 1616, and after the appearance of the first folio of Jonson's works, the latter poet produced a comedy of devil-lore, confessedly to rival Dekker's *If It Be Not a Good Play* and *The Merry Devil of Edmonton*. Moreover, while *The*

---

[11] *An Account of English Dramatic Poets*, 122.
[12] *The Faery Queen*, iii, 9. 10.
[13] Dodsley, *Old Plays*, ed. 1874, viii, 393.
[14] See especially *A Knack to Know a Knave*, ibid., vi, 509.

Devil Is an Ass is conceived with a measure of that bold originality and mingling of minute realism with fanciful invention which is, in stronger degree elsewhere, Jonson's, *The Marriage of Belphegor* must certainly have suggested to the English dramatist his general design. Pug, the lesser devil, out of a childlike curiosity and ambition to extend the dominion of hell, seeks the world for one day in the face of dissuasive advice of the more experienced great devil, Satan. In the body of a lately hanged cutpurse and in clothes stolen from a servant Pug seeks employment of a rich old fool and makes a few abortive advances to intimacy with mankind. But he is repulsed, beaten, and cheated at every turn, and in the end escapes being whipped to Tyburn at the tail of a cart for the theft of the suit of clothes he wears only by reason of the expiration of his day on earth. It is a far cry from the dignity and overpowering terror of the conception of Faustus to pitiful Pug on his knees to his master, who will not believe him to be a real devil, although honestly assured of the fact. Drolly pathetic are the poor devil's last moments, sighing in Newgate for midnight to set him free from his chains and restore him to "his holidays in hell."[15]

Turning back to the latter days of Queen Elizabeth, in Dekker's loosely constructed but poetical comedy of *Old Fortunatus,* printed in 1600, we find a tale of folk-lore very different in its original intention from *Faustus,* and yet strongly affected by that tragedy. There is reason to believe that Dekker's play as we

[15] Gifford, *Jonson,* v, 132, 135.

have it is the result of the revision of a comedy dealing with Fortunatus and his inexhaustible purse, well known to the stage as early as February, 1596. Whether this "first part" was Dekker's or another's, that dramatist revised the whole work, probably adding the adventures of the sons of Fortunatus in November, 1599; and, the play being unexpectedly ordered for court, further added the poetical masque-like scenes which depict the strife of Vice and Virtue, later in the same year.[16] In Dekker's hands the old fairy tale of the gift of Fortune and the wishing-cap, which carries the wearer whither he will, is transmuted from its original frank worldliness into a theme of moral gravity by the allegorical contention of Virtue and Vice and by the emphasis which is laid on the folly of Fortunatus in his choice of wealth, with the discord and doom which the inheritance of it entails on his sons. Could Dekker have written always as he wrote in the best scenes of this beautiful play, he could well challenge a place beside the greatest poets of his age.

"There were no real fairies before Shakespeare's, what were called 'fairies' have existed ever since stories were told to wide-eyed listeners round a winter's fire. But these are not the fairies of Shakespeare, nor the fairies of to-day. They are the fairies of Grimm's mythology. Our fairies are spirits of another sort, but unless they wear Shakespeare's livery they are counterfeit."[17] The truth of this statement must appear to

[16] *Henslowe's Diary*, ii, 179.
[17] H. H. Furness, *Variorum Shakespeare*, x, p. xxiv.

anyone who will be at the pains to turn to the innumerable "sources" of Shakespeare's fairy-lore which the indefatigable industry of commentators has unearthed. Oberon, the *deus ex machina* of the old romance of *Huon of Bordeaux*, although he possesses some of the features of Shakespeare's fairy king, is a dwarf and a mortal;[18] his namesake in Greene's drama on King James IV is little more than the presenter of a series of dumb shows and the coryphæus of a "round" of fairies, who dance jigs and hornpipes wholly extraneous to the action of the play.[19]   And a perusal of *The Faery Queen* which had stopped well short of the third book could alone have misled anyone into the supposition that the Elfe and Fay, "of whom all faeryes spring and fetch their lignage," have anything in common with Cobweb, Moth, and Mustardseed. Shakespeare refined the elves and goblins of folk-lore to a diminutiveness and daintiness beyond the reach of the gross imaginations of the countryside, as he transmuted the fays of the bookish lands of "faerie" into a charming and fanciful reality.   Robin Goodfellow and Queen Mab meet without incongruity, and Puck and the gossamer-winged attendants on Bottom shade imperceptibly into the airy tenants of the exuberant fancy of Mercutio and the haunting music and invisible spells of *The Tempest*.

[18] See *Huon of Bordeaux*, ed. Early English Text Society (1882), 60, 267.

[19] *The Scottish History of King James IV, Greene*, ed. Grosart, xiii, 205.

A Midsummer Night's Dream produced a profound impression on the poetic imagination of the day, and thenceforth (to say nothing of non-dramatic productions such as Drayton's *Nymphidia* and the fairy-lore of the pastoralists) scenes introducing elves and fairies enter not infrequently into popular plays as well as into performances at court. Thus in the confused romantic comedy of intrigue, *The Wisdom of Doctor Dodipol,* which must have been written very soon after Shakespeare's play, fairies usher in a banquet and an enchanter exorcises spells on wood-wandering lovers not dissimilar to those of Puck. In *The Maid's Metamorphosis,* printed in 1600, the fairy element also obtrudes in several very pretty songs,[20] although the play is of a pastoral and mythological cast in the manner of Lyly and was formerly inaccurately ascribed to him. Even into the midst of so melodramatic a performance as the quasi-historical tragedy *Lust's Dominion* Oberon and his fairy rout are lugged to warn a character of her impending death.[21] Shakespeare employed mock fairies in the delightful masquerade which brings about at once the punishment of Falstaff and the *dénouement* of *The Merry Wives of Windsor;* [22] while later, in 1610, the dainty fairy-lore of *A Midsummer Night's Dream* expands into the imaginative world of the supernatural which girdles the enchanted island of Prospero, a world wherein the ro-

[20] Bullen, *Old English Plays* (1884), iii, 135; i, 127.

[21] This play may have been written as early as 1600; the passage alluded to is iii, 2.

[22] V, v, 41.

mantic and the grotesque, ethereal spirit and mortality in its nobility and in its sensual grossness unite in a perfect harmony which only Shakespeare could have infused into such discordant materials.

But Shakespeare's poetic and fanciful transfiguration of popular fairy-lore was not the only literary and dramatic treatment of the fairies of his age. The diligent researches into primitive and bookish mythology so confidently applied to Shakespeare's free creations of the supernatural world are far more significant and fruitful when applied to the fairies of Ben Jonson; and here, as elsewhere, that learned man and poet of a wholly admirable talent stands in striking contrast to the brilliant, imaginative, and all-conquering genius of him who alone of all Jonson's contemporaries could equal and surpass him. Jonson's contributions to fairy-lore in dramatic form are included in *The Satyr,* " a particular entertainment of the Queen and Prince at Althorpe . . . 1603, as they came first into the Kingdom; " *Oberon, the Faery Prince,* a Masque of Prince Henry's, 1610; and the character of Puck in *The Sad Shepherd.* Jonson's fairies, like the Irish "other people," do not seem to have been conspicuously distinguishable for their small size; [23] and, as might be expected from their employment in masques, are notable, like those of Greene, for their dancing, and to this they add a very pretty quality in song.[24] Jon-

---

[23] The " lesser faies " of *Oberon* were represented by noble children; the greater hence presumably, by adults.
[24] See especially the songs in *Oberon.*

son's Puck is no " merry wanderer of the night," but
is surnamed "Hairy" and debased to attendance on
the Witch of Paplewick; whilst to Queen Mab, in vast
discrepancy to the delicate and pampered royalty of
Titania, are ascribed the tricksy pranks of will-o'-the-
wisp, moon-calf, and household elf. It was reserved
in much later times to Jonson's witty, reckless, and
godless "son," Thomas Randolph, to laugh the fairies
off the stage. In his fine pastoral drama *Amyntas*,
published in 1638, Randolph employs a mock fairy
motif to enhance the lighter comedy scenes of his play.
In the course of it Jocastus, a fantastic shepherd and
"fairy knight," and Mopsus, a foolish augur, carry
on much satirical discourse concerning fairies and
fairy-lore; and in the end contrive to rob an orchard
by means of a "bevy of fairies " who for some reason
best known to their author sing, though prettily, only
in Latin. Told to " go love some fairy lady," Mopsus
replies:

> How, Jocastus,
> Marry a puppet? wed a mote i' th' sun?
> Go look a wife in nutshells? Woo a gnat,
> That's nothing but a voice? No, no, Jocastus,
> I must have flesh and blood, ...
> A fig for fairies! [25]

The fairies dwell in pleasant regions of fancy and
their drama is comedy. Witchcraft in its grotesqueness, its horror, and its pathos occupies, as has well
been said, " a field debatable, in a way unparalleled

[25] " Amyntas, or the Impossible Dowry." *Works of Randolph* (1875),
i, 278.

between tragedy and comedy." In a sermon preached before the queen in 1572, John Jewell, wise and pious bishop that he was, declared:

> Witches and sorcerers, within these last few yeeres, are marvellously increased within this your Grace's realme. These eies have seene most evident and manefest marks of their wickedness. . . . Wherefore, your poore subjects most humble petition unto your Highnesse, is that the laws touching such malefactors, may be put in due execution.[26]

This may be taken as a measure of the popular belief in witchcraft, which among the political and religious difficulties that beset the reigns of the later Tudors, from a harmless white magic, useful for the discovery of things lost, for the mixture of love philters, or for effecting simple cures, came to be regarded as a dreadful and alarming evil, spreading like the plague and blasting with death in this world and with damnation in the world to come the unhappy creatures who fell under suspicion of traffic in it. To the Elizabethan playgoer the apparition of Mephistophilis to Faustus or the conjurings of the wizard, Bolingbroke, and Margery Jourdain, dealers in the supernatural in *2 Henry VI*, seemed the natural representation of things universally known to be true; and the extraordinary reversal of the military successes of Henry V and of Talbot by the French, a foe habitually despised and beaten, could be accounted for in no other wise than by the acceptance of the English tradition that Joan of Arc had been justly tried and burnt for a witch.[27]

[26] Quoted in Scot, *Discoverie of Witchcraft*, Introduction, p. xxxii.
[27] *2 Henry VI*, v, iii.

The plays of the age of Elizabeth are full of allusions to these popular superstitions, from the allegorical representation of the practices against Elizabeth's life in a work of Dekker,[28] to the farcical situation of Falstaff, disguised as the Wise Woman of Brentford.[29] But it was not until King James ascended the throne and gave to the popular belief in witchcraft the sanction of the royal opinion, that the witch, as such, enters as a motive into the fabric of English plays. Heywood, Shakespeare, Dekker, Middleton, and Ford, all deal with witchcraft; imaginatively, realistically, jocularly, pathetically, in only one case — Heywood's *Wise Woman of Hogsdon* — in the least skeptically.[30] Jonson, who repudiated and satirized the followers of alchemy and astrology, hesitated to attack the more terrible superstitions of witchcraft, but represents his witches in *The Masque of Queens,* 1609, with a circumstantial attention to every coarse and unseemly detail and a display of erudition, classic and modern, which must have delighted the grossness and pedantry alike of the royal author of a treatise on demonology.

The witches of *Macbeth* preceded as they surpassed all other representation of their kind on the stage: for the little that went before, Lyly's *Mother Bombie*[31] and the examples already cited, were neither vital nor closely interwoven in the tissues of the play. But de-

---

[28] *The Whore of Babylon* (1604).

[29] *Merry Wives,* iv, ii.

[30] The wise woman of Hogsdon is little more than a female quack doctor. See an interesting passage on the " wise women " of the time, ii, 1. *Heywood's Dramatic Works* (1874), v, 292.

[31] First printed in 1594.

spite the fidelity with which Shakespeare followed his
source, as was his wont, and notwithstanding a certain
incongruity which the supererogatory queen of witches
Hecate brings into the imaginative conception of the
three Weird Sisters, the witches of *Macbeth* rise so far
above the wretched hags and obscene *succubae* of popular demonology, so ally themselves on the one hand
with the cosmic forces of nature and so vividly represent the visible symbolical form of subjective human
depravity on the other, that they, no more than Shakespeare's fairies, can be accepted as really illustrative
of the popular belief of the time.

For the popular dramatic exposition of witchcraft
we must then turn to other authors. Jonson's Witch
of Paplewick is possessed of most of the malignant and
repulsive features of her kind. She assumes the shape
of a raven and again of innocent Maid Marian, to fo-
ment mischief. She is hunted at full cry by a band of
huntsmen who mistake her for a hare, and is about to
be represented " with her spells, threads and images,"
when Jonson's fragment abruptly comes to an end.[32]
Even more repulsively realistic are the hags who enact
the antimasque of *The Masque of Queens* already
mentioned above. These witches are described as is-
suing "with a kind of hollow and infernal music"
from " an ugly hell," " all differently attired, some with
rats on their head, some on their shoulders; others
with ointment-pots at their girdles; all with spindles,
timbrels, rattles, or other venefical instruments, making a confused noise, with strange gestures." Amid

[32] *The Sad Shepherd,* iii, 2, *Gifford Jonson,* vi, 283.

charms and incantations admirable for their grotesque and grewsome horror and suggestiveness, the
" Dame " or queen of witches enters, " naked-armed,
bare-footed, her frock tucked, her hair knotted and
folded with vipers; in her hands a torch made of a
dead man's arm, lighted, girded with a snake; " and
the roll is called, the witches responding to such names
as Credulity, Impudence, Slander, Bitterness, Rage,
and other abstractions.[33]

In *The Witch*, by Thomas Middleton (of uncertain
date, but assuredly written after *Macbeth*), that ready
playwright grafted on a romantic tale of Belleforest a
story of witchcraft derived through Scot's *Discoverie*
from Nider's *Formicarius*,[34] a work written in Latin
by a German. The original version of this latter story
concerns the unholy doings of three wizards and their
successive practices in their craft. Middleton, with a
dramatist's instinct, changed their sex, united their
adventures, and linked them with the witchcrone of
antiquity by naming one of their number Hecate, besides giving to their incantations an influential part in
determining the course of the play. The witch name
Hecate thus occurs in both Shakespeare's and Middleton's play; and likenesses of phrase have been discovered in the witch scenes of the two dramas, radically
different as the governing conceptions of these ministers of evil appear in the two productions. Moreover it
has been thought that the extraneousness and contra-

[33] See *ibid.*, vii, 108, 112.
[34] See Herford, *Literary Relations*, 233. Book V of the *Formicarius*
treats " De Maleficis," etc.

dictory nature of Shakespeare's Hecate as compared
with her sister witches is to be explained by assuming
an interpolation by Middleton or another hand in a
play originally free from this and other like blemishes.
The last word has been said on this comparison by
Charles Lamb, in a passage which quotation can never
stale:

[Shakespeare's] witches, [he tells us], are distinguished from the witches of Middleton by essential differences. "These are creatures to whom man or
woman plotting some dire mischief might resort for
occasional consultation. Those originate deeds of
blood, and begin bad impulses to men. From the moment that their eyes first met with Macbeth's, he
is spellbound. That meeting sways his destiny. He
can never break the fascination. These witches can
hurt the body: those have power over the soul. Hecate
in Middleton has a son, a low buffoon: the hags of
Shakespeare have neither child of their own, nor seem
to be descended from any parent. They are foul
anomalies, of whom we know not whence they are
sprung, nor whether they have beginning or ending.
As they are without human passions, so they seem
to be without human relations. They come with
thunder and lightning, and vanish to airy music. This
is all we know of them. Except Hecate they have
no names: which heightens their mysteriousness.
Their names, and some of the properties which
Middleton has given to his hags, excite smiles. The
Weird Sisters are serious things. Their presence cannot coexist with mirth. But, in a lesser degree, the

Witches of Middleton are fine creations. They raise jars, jealousies, strifes, 'like a thick scurf o'er life.' " [35]

There remain two remarkable plays in which English witchcraft is sketched from life. Their treatment in this place neither their late date nor the realism which allies them with the domestic drama whose theme is everyday life could excuse, were it not for the presence in both of a certain element of grotesqueness and wonder and the humane spirit that suggests, even if it does not portray, the pathos of the situation of these unhappy traffickers in evil. *The Witch of Edmonton* was most likely first acted towards the end of the reign of King James, and is assigned on its title page to the " well esteemed poets, William Rowley, Thomas Dekker, John Ford, etc." The play is grounded on a prose account of one Elizabeth Sawyer of Islington, who was executed in 1621 for witchcraft; and belongs in its general theme to the striking series of tragedies that deal with domestic unhappiness and consequent crime. Mother Sawyer, a wretched and poverty-stricken old woman, is driven to commerce with the supernatural in revenge for outrageous and wanton ill treatment on the part of her neighbors. A devil in shape of a black dog surprises her in one of her paroxysms of impotent cursing, exacts from her the usual pledge of her soul, and becomes her " familiar." [36] Her feud with the neighborhood continues until, deserted by her evil spirit, her hut is set afire and

[35] *Specimens of English Dramatic Poets* (ed. 1893), i, 271.
[36] *The Witch of Edmonton*, ii, 1.

she is arraigned and convicted of her many acts of spite and mischief. Forbiddingly coarse as are many of the details of this story of vulgar malice, the character of Mother Sawyer is conceived with a sympathy for the miserable old hag, with a touch of pathos and an apprehension of the moral responsibility of her persecutors which is surprising in view of the circumstance that neither her actual possession by her grotesque familiar spirit nor the supernatural quality of her traffic is called into question for a moment.

The Late Lancashire Witches was printed in 1634 as the work of Thomas Heywood and Richard Brome,[37] its source the notorious trials for witchcraft of 1633 in the county named. Indeed, to judge from the epilogue, the composition of this play must have followed so close on the events that its influence in forestalling the judgment of the courts which tried these unfortunate creatures can scarcely be considered negligible. Attention has been called to the repetition of a familiar *motif* of Heywood's in the main event of *The Lancashire Witches*. Like Mistress Franklin, the woman killed with kindness, like Wincott's wife in *The English Traveller*, Mistress Generous, the wife of an honorable man, is led astray, here not by an earthly lover, but by the powers of darkness to which she pledges her soul and becomes a witch. In the other two plays the erring wife is magnanimously, even tenderly, treated; here the enormity of the crime demanded another *dénouement*. *The Lancashire Witches* is a mine of cur-

[37] *Dramatic Works of Heywood*, iv, 167.

rent witch-lore, with its transformations of supposedly respectable housewives into midnight hags and thence into cats or supernatural jades that traverse miraculous distances, with its grotesque malice, unhallowed revels and wanton breeding of strife. The pathos is not for the witches, but for the upright husband deceived by his witch-wife, whose repentance is feigned. At length she is discovered by the loss of her hand in one of her midnight escapades while transformed into the shape of a cat; and she is delivered over to justice by her sorrowful and offended lord, but without a qualm of conscience as to the rectitude of his act. *The Lancashire Witches* is an excellent example of the journalist's instinct that sees and instantly appropriates to present use material of current interest. It is terrible to think that the fate of some of the unfortunate thousands who perished in the seventeenth century accused of these loathsome and impossible crimes may have hung on the reception of this circumstantial representation of their alleged misdeeds on the popular stage.

The dreadful compact of Faustus and the pleasing white magic of Friar Bacon were succeeded by the *diablerie* of Grim the Collier and Friar Rush, and by the savage irony of *The Devil is an Ass*. The terpsichorean fairies of Jonson's masques followed the poetical and fanciful sprites of *A Midsummer Night's Dream*, to be followed in turn by the satiric elves of Randolph. In each of these cases the general absorption of the supernatural as a motive in Elizabethan drama is satirical; for satire and romance are things absolutely alien and incompatible. With witchcraft the tale is different. From a vague and indefinable element of the preternatural in the wizards of old romance, this *motif* dilated under the hand of Shakespeare into the mysterious horror and spiritual terror which the doings and the prophecies of the witches in *Macbeth* inspire; only to dwindle through Middleton's half successful imitation of the Weird Sisters, and through the grotesque hags of Jonson's masques to compassion for the maunderings of Mother Sawyer and contempt for the lewd gambols and physical transformations of Mall Spencer and Mistress Generous, the Lancashire witches.

XI

SHAKESPEARE IN TWENTY MINUTES

SOMETHING about Shakespeare; and not more than twenty minutes of it: such are my specifications; and it will become me faithfully to adhere to them. Something about Shakespeare! Well, I might tell you that it was William Shakespeare and not William Harvey who discovered the circulation of blood. Or, let me see, I might declare that Queen Elizabeth was really " the dark lady " intended in the *Sonnets:* not of course a black lady, nor a brunette lady — Elizabeth's hair was notoriously " golden "; which is Elizabethan for red — assuredly not an obscure lady; least of all, let us hope, a shady lady; but merely a lady unwilling to be known. Both these statements, so far as I know, are new about Shakespeare; but unhappily neither is true; and the world is far too full of skilful lying for me to hope to thrive conspicuously in that delicate art. Again, I might tell you that Shakespeare made more money out of literature — that is out of the success of his plays — than anybody until the novels of Sir Walter Scott and the history of Lord Macaulay; that although he tried to prevent publication to protect his acting rights, more editions of his plays were printed in his lifetime than of any playwright of his time whatsoever; further I might tell you that we know a great deal more about Shakespeare than we know about any man of his age who was situated as he was situated in life, a player, a dramatist and little connected with patrons or the court except through his works. But all this, while abundantly true, has been so often repeated in refutation of error or otherwise, that novelty can assuredly not be claimed for it. Wherefore the inference, that I at least can hope to say nothing about Shakespeare which combines verity with the charm of novelty; being in which unhappy state, I throw myself upon the reader's mercy.

I am told that clergymen sadly at a loss for a text and wanting something sensational, which even clergymen sometimes do, often preach on what they think would happen should He who drove out the money-lenders — let us say it with all reverence — should He come to Wall Street. Unfortunately for any claim as to originality on my part, even with this cue, Mr. Don Marquis, that master columnist, has already told us what would happen if Shakespeare should come to New York. How the reporters would swarm about him — of whom some of them perhaps would have heard — to ask him how he liked America before he had more than seen the goddess of liberty enlightening New York harbor! How Mr. Baker, sometime of Harvard, now translated to Yale, would explain the precise manner in which plays were successfully made at Cambridge and are now to be made even more successfully at New Haven; and Mr. Phelps of Yale and the Philadelphia Forum, at a very dry dinner given by — perhaps the Bacon Society of Staten Island — would introduce Mr. Belasco, "the Shakespeare of America," to Mr. Shakespeare, "the British Belasco." I do not remember whether Mr. Marquis told of the charming bobbed reporterette, who fixing the gaze of ingenuous childhood on the august Shakespearean countenance, asked: "Now, my dear Mr. Shakespeare, do tell me, did you really intend to make Hamlet mad? Or did he just run mad without your intending it?"

However, a more pertinent matter for us is what would Shakespeare do, how would be behave, if he were the fortunate guest of the English Speaking Union to-night, meeting in the splendid capital of a new land far beyond his "still vext Bermoothes," meeting, too, so many who admire and praise him, howsoever little some of us really do read him. He would come, I should think, "in his habit as he lived," and not with so much as a wig to cover his fine intellectual baldness. And would we, if he did, be so irreligious as to smile at the quaintness of his slashed doublet, his starched ruff, his bombast trousers and the provence roses of ribbon on his shoes? While he, on his part, might wonder at "our customary suits of solemn black" and inquire whose death among the great we are so protractedly commemorating in our modern Puritan mourning. Courteous our guest would be to all; for is he not "the gentle Shakespeare?" And solicitous of our opinion and good will, often using phrases such as "What you will, kind sir," or "As you like it, ladies."

And our guest would punctiliously respect "degree, order and place," however he might be astonished to find such things in honor in America: America! of which, however, he will of course have heard the loud report even in Elysium. He would understand and approve, I am sure, the English Speaking Union and whatever makes for kindliness and brotherhood; and he would rejoice that his works should be so strong a bond between two mighty nations. I am sure that he would be indulgent to some of our guesses about him, though heaven forbid that he should hear some things that are said; and, even though now a wraith, he might resent some of our efforts to prove that he never existed. He would understand, perhaps with some difficulty, our unlubricated feast of reason and our potationless flow of soul; for he was accustomed to those full flowing nights at the Mermaid Tavern where, it will be remembered, he "such clusters had as made him nobly wild, not mad " — whatever may be said on those occasions of Ben Jonson. And he would be comforted in the recollection, which is all the comfort we can offer him.

And what would our august guest think of contemporary drama? The man who invoked, in his auditors', imagination's inward eye to body forth the vasty fields of France, would laugh at the pedantic notion that his plays are best performed forever in the tiny "wooden O's," on the restricted little platforms, which he alone knew. Shakespeare would be delighted and eager to welcome each help to the artistic production of the drama; the picture stage, variety and change of scenery, women in the charm of youth and beauty in place of the squeaking boys in women's rôles which he alone knew. Superior lighting, fitness and elegance of costume, all this would please him; but I think he would miss the beauty and flow of his musical blank verse on our stage. He might wonder at the stress we lay on setting and stage carpentry; and I am sure that he would object to the idiocy of destroying the continuity of a fine play with the interruption of irrelevant music. Depend upon it, Shakespeare would recognize the futility of our drama with a purpose and the inanity of our drama without a purpose; and I doubt if he would welcome the cubistic symbolism of nowhere draping an incomprehensible nowhen, or approve either a *King Lear* tethered to the setting of Stonehenge or a *Hamlet* a-see-saw on a flight of stairs.[1] Moreover, what could Shakespeare have thought of this much-abused Prince, tuxedo-clad, and of little Ophelia clipped, not only as to her lines, but likewise as to her skirts and her hair?

Most great writers see men and things either as they are or as they are transfigured; some — and these are seldom really great — see them in their unhappy lapses into disease and crime, and see them only thus. A peculiarity of Shakespeare consists in the fact that he sees the world all but simultaneously in all its possible ways and leads us unerringly through the intricacies of life in which it is so easy to go astray. He is apt to give us a clew, a chorus or commentator in some one of his personages who acts to keep us straight, lest we be-

[1] See the *Theatre Magazine*, 1926.

come distraught in the action. Plain unimaginative Horatio; Paulina, devoted to the service of her lady Hermione; Pesanio, as devoted to Imogen; Kent, faithful to Lear. Each is offered as a species of horizon line, above or below which the passion of the play may plunge, but which steadfastly maintains for us our moral equilibrium.

There are really many interesting things to repeat about Shakespeare, however they may not startle with their originality. Have you happened to notice, for example, how his attitude towards his personages changes with his own years and growth in experience? The young people of *Love's Labour's Lost* and *The Two Gentlemen of Verona* are gentle folk as a country-bred lad sees them from afar with a help of the plays of the court writer, John Lyly. Richard III is a super-man or rather a supermonster — the two are much the same — drawn partly from history as she is miswritten and from Marlowe's ideas of a hero. In *Romeo and Juliet* the author's sympathies are wholly with the lovers, and of course he takes us with him. It has been well said that Friar Laurence and Old Capulet both talk in the manner in which young men think that old men talk. Indeed there might be something to be said for the latter old fellow, crusty though he was. How would you like to have your little girl of fourteen philandering on a balcony by moonlight, with the lackadaisical boy of that hateful Mr. Montague, next door, with whom you have just had a personal altercation? Wouldn't the minx deserve at the least expostulation? In the later plays the interest centers in maturer personages. I take it that Benedick is no boy, but the senior of Orlando; while Duke Orsino is older still. As to the ladies — they are always young. In the later plays, however, we have such personages as that splendid Roman matron, the mother of Coriolanus, and that loveliest figure of elderly womanhood, the Countess of Roussilon. Even Cleopatra was no "March chick," — but who am I to hazard a guess as to the age of any woman?

By the bye, is there anyone who can tell me why it is that Shakespeare's heroines are, so many of them, orphans, or at least motherless? Viola, Portia, have neither father nor mother alive; Isabella and her miserable brother; Helena, despite the lady who "mothers" her, are in like plight. Claudio's Hero is furnished with a mother by name in the opening stage direction of *Much Ado:* that is if you do not read in a modern sophisticated edition. This lady is called "Innogen, wife to Leonato," and a veritable poet once wrote a very charming sonnet to her.[2] But she drops out of the play without a word, so that Beatrice shall not have so much even as an aunt to reprove her wayward tongue. Imogen, in *Cymbeline*, has a wicked step-mother after the manner of orthodox fairy tales. As to the tragedies, Cordelia, Desdemona, Ophelia, all are motherless. Juliet had both father and mother and was little the better for it, poor child. Perish the thought that Shakespeare should have balked at handling the mother-in-law. And yet, whatever the reason, Shakespeare's heroes are started in life free from that

[2] S. Weir Mitchell, *Complete Poems*, 1914, p. 380.

187

handicap. Even Petruchio, who perhaps might have won out, was in justice not served with such odds in his task of taming the shrew. Shakespeare is fair minded and could not brook two against one, and that one only a miserable man.

Another notable thing, we might call it, is the variety of the tempo of the plays: the tempo, as in music. *Hamlet* is a leisurely tragedy; it expands slowly, gradually, inevitably, like the slow processes of Fate, only hastening into a swirl of engulfment in the catastrophe which sucks down all. *Othello* is of a brisker action — for Iago's machinations are like those of a busy, incessant spider; but still the movement of *Othello* is not hasty. *Macbeth* gathers force and speed, but for the delay for contrast in the long scene in England. But *King Lear* is of a torrential swiftness. Even the comedies vary from the allegretto of *As You Like It,* to the allegro of *Much Ado About Nothing* and the presto of *The Taming of the Shrew.*

Everybody learns at school about the "honorable men" of Antony's famous speech over the dead body of Caesar, with the transmutation of that phrase by repetition into a terrible irony. But not so many may have observed that Shakespeare elsewhere uses this method more extendedly. "Honest" is the theme word of the tragedy of *Othello;* "seeming," or the pretence of respectable appearances, as we should say, is the theme word for *Measure for Measure.* I have counted forty recurrences of "honest" in the former play; from "honest Iago," reiterated until the irony of it overpowers us, to the despairing Desdemona's agonizing cry: "I hope my noble lord esteems me honest," in which the word means something very different. In the other play the whole action turns on the Duke's purpose: "Hence shall we see, if power change purpose, what our seemers be." The art of Shakespeare is subtle in small as well as in great things, and he who thinks that he can find three ideas in a phrase where Shakespeare sowed only two, is but a vain man. Little do we need to philosophise on Shakespeare and look for esoteric significances in his direct and open words. If we seek in humble wise to understand him, we shall have a sufficient reward for our pains; for to know what he really has said, to be sustained by his wisdom and elevated by his poetry, ennobled by his exalted view of man, these things are better than any commentary of yours or mine on his want of a knowledge of modern science, the unorthodoxy of his religion — thank God for that — or the inadequacy of his art to size up in every paltry particular to what some theorist has found out that it ought to be.

The theorists are the only people who are troubled about Shakespeare; the rest of us merely enjoy him. If you nourish a suspicion that the Shakespearean figures are eked out with cyphers, I commend the study of logarithms as likely to prove even more fruitful than these plays. If you are dying to be improved and uplifted by moral injunctions and disquisitions, be there not sermons in this much bepreached world? And if you are mad about psychic matters, I am told that Sir Oliver Lodge is a very diverting author, though he may not know as much about the next world as the

father of Hamlet or even Polonius, though Polonius
in all likelihood is now quartered in quite a different
place. Shakespeare is to be judged as a dramatist, a
poet, an artist; and is not this enough without testing
him as an alienist, a gospeller or a spiritist?

The great Tolstoi quarreled with Shakespeare because he did not write like the Bible and add to Revela-
tions. As to Mr. Bernard Shaw, another objector to
the great dramatist, of course even Shakespeare does
not write like Mr. Shaw. It is not really Mr. Shaw
who invented "unpleasant plays." *Troilus* and *Cressida* and *Measure for Measure* are as unpleasant and
as wholesome as any play need be: the unpleasantness
need not extend to the author. For Shakespeare knew
that in the picture of this unhappy-happy world in
which we have to live, as in any good dinner, there
must be the sweet, the salt, the bitter and the sour.
And he also knew that you can spoil a good dinner by
a long grace before it and that all the gustatory art and
the hygienics of appetite are as nothing to the dinner itself. I am not quite sure that one of the best
things about Shakespeare is not his reticence. Like
the gentleman that he is, he neither discusses politics
nor religion. As to the former there are people who
say that he worshiped kings. Do the pictures of foiled
King John, incompetent Henry VI, vacillating Richard II and the monster Richard Crookback look like
worship? Is gross Henry VIII a saint or calculating
Henry IV a hero? And these form the majority of
Shakespeare's kings. By the same token, Shakespeare
is often accused of contempt for the crowd and con-

descension to the common man. Are crowds steadfast, cleanly, reasonable and to be trusted? Which of us has a congenital yearning for the submerged tenth? And is not Shakespeare really as fair, if not fairer, than you or I to the man in the street? As to religion, Shakespeare is tender to priests of the old faith and respectful to the oracle at Delphi. That delightful man and sound scholar, Sir Walter Raleigh, alas that we must say late professor of literature at Oxford, used to remark that it is to the credit of human discernment that nobody has as yet called Shakespeare a Puritan. Depend upon it, somebody will, and with no great difference in the measure of his folly to that of some who have called him by other hard names. Can it be that Shakespeare is so veritably of the right religion that you and I, each in his diverse faith, feel sure that he belongs only in our own orthodox camp? The very crown of Shakespeare's reticence, however, lies in the almost unparalleled circumstance among writers that he talks little of his art and not at all about himself. These matters he has considerately left to his commentators and the critics, this being, alas, what the lawyers call " an exhibit " of what we make of it.

Lastly, as I never remember to have said anything about Shakespeare anywhere without being drawn aside by somebody and asked in confidence my opinion as to whether he wrote his own plays, I shall forestall this anxious inquiry here with a public answer. Like so many better things, this opinion of mine is taken from *Life*. However, as I myself gave it *Life* I shall offer no apology for the query.

WHO WROTE SHAKESPEARE? [3]

M'sieur Lefranc, who hails from Paris,
Following a Mr. Harris,
    More or less,
Believes that Shakespeare's dramas are by
William Stanley Earl of Darby:
    That's his guess.

M'sieur Demblon, who likewise French is,
Holds, of dates and facts, such wrenches
    Under ban;
Sure as Elsinore's not Jutland,
Roger Manners Earl of Rutland
    Is the man.

These are foreign theories, Gaully;
A New Yorker thought that Raleigh
    Filled the myth;
Colonel Watterson says " Marlowe,"
And a certain Mr. Barlow
    Thinks 'twas Smith.

Was it Dawes? forgotten Cox? Ford?
Mr. Looney swears Lord Oxford
    Slung the ink;
" J. T. Looney," though illumey,
Sounds a wee bit nom de plumey,
    Don't you think?

You may believe it Oxford, Lyly,
Rutland, that some other Willy

[3] Reprinted by permission of the Publishers from *Life*, September 20,
1920.

Writ these plays;
But you mustn't think that Bacon
Was a poet or could take on
Such bad ways.

Francis really had no eye for
Drama, what he loved was cypher,
Law — and pelf.
Yet these plays got written. Come now!
Could it be Will cribbed them, somehow,
From himself?

XII

AMERICA'S ELIZABETHAN HERITAGE

IT IS MY happy vocation to live in daily touch with the writings of a great age, to seek somewhat to understand the circumstance and conditions of the times of the great Queen Elizabeth, whose subjects did a bewildering number of remarkable things in nearly everything in which a man can be remarkable, and produced incidentally the greatest literature, in all the qualities that make literature great, which the world has as yet brought forth. My shop is a delightful one and full of curiosities and rarities; but it is also, let me hope, a shop open to daylight and the sun, and significant, in that what it holds is related to the rest of mankind, and especially, I believe, to this new, free, hopeful, careless, blundering and beloved America of ours. It is where the crossroads meet and peoples fuse that history is made, and new nations. Periclean Athens, republican Rome, Elizabethan England, and now our new America: man is always man and our inheritances are strong upon us. In the bewildering make-up of what we denominate America, it is not always easy to unravel three or four threads in a tangled skein. But our government, our political ideals, our procedure at law, the forms which our Christianity has prevailingly taken, our social manners and customs are fundamentally English, despite all foreign tinges and tinctures and, being English, were sometime derivable from conditions and characteristics intrinsic in the days of the great queen. My topic, in a word, is America's Elizabethan Heritage.

A few years since, during the war, a clever and somewhat exasperating writer put forth a book entitled *The American Language.* In it he carefully contrasted literary and cultivated English, as written and spoken by those who speak it best in England, with our American tongue as " she is spoke " in what used to be called the Bowery in New York's East Side; and of course he found a marked, if not an appalling, contrast. Somebody has recently translated the Bible into Chicagoese, that the hooligans of that leading criminal city of the world may come by reading to repentance. This " language " is quite unlike the English of the *Authorized Version,* and perhaps, outside of Chicago, to cultivated people a foreign tongue. And this is all very well. But why should not our Mr. Mencken have contrasted the cultivated speech of, let us say Boston or cosmopolitan New York, with the costermongers' jargon of East London or that of the Southampton dockyards? The contrast would have been at least as great and the comparison quite as enlightening. Differences are obvious; my concern is with similarities, not diversities, whether of trait or of long usage. It is the inheritances of common traits, yearnings and aspirations that make a people one and perpetuate in new nations, sprung from a common stock, the qualities which endure. And it matters very little that the travelling English "book luggage" while we "check baggage," that they ascend tall buildings by way of "lifts" while we use for taller buildings "elevators," or that we prefer a Latin "exit" to the plain "way out."

A strong stock, like that of the Anglo-Saxon, has almost an infinite power of absorption. Into the British Isles it came, taking up the best of the civilization of four hundred years of the rule of Rome, enriching its blood with the Celt, dignifying it with the Scandinavian, pushing into the western seas what it could not make its own. In our America, too, we have preserved to a surprising degree this power to assimilate, this vigorous Anglo-Saxon racial digestion. We have taken much metal in at the doors of this our American mint, not all of it bullion. And the mighty machines that are stamping it indiscriminately with the face of the Goddess of Liberty, to make it current in the realm, groan and strain at their work. But it would take an alchemist, not a political process, to transmute all this strange metal into the gold of veritable American citizenship, and it is no wonder that some of it lies heavy and of little worth on our hands. However as yet, despite the anxieties of Mr. Mencken, Japanese is not the language of Hollywood, nor Yiddish wholly that of Manhattan. In words of the well-known reply of Lowell to the impertinence of an English questioner concerning certain New England idioms, "We had, sir, unhappily, when we came to America, nothing better to bring with us than the language of Chaucer and Shakespeare."

Whatever the grafts and experiments that have come after, ours is the British ancestral tree, ours as much as that of the veriest cockney who has never trod any streets except those of London: and the essential traits of our inheritance run as rich and red in our veins as in those of any one of our stock. I have never been able to accept with patience the notion that in reading the great English classics — Milton, Dr. Johnson, Sir Walter Scott, Carlyle or Browning — we Americans are dealing with alien authors. Whatever may be true of the warriors and the politicians, the intelligence, the imagination, the social lore and the poetry of England belong quite as fully to us as to any Celtic-Saxon-Norman, Scotch or Irish Englishman still resident by circumstances in the British Isles. And correspondingly the accident that some of our poetry, our fiction, has been written in our Cambridge by Longfellow, in London by Henry James, or by our Mr. Frost in the hills of New Hampshire, can in no wise imperil its standing as a part integral of that great ocean of achievement, properly to be designated English literature and not narrowly as merely American. The laws of primogeniture, in a word, do not run as to letters. The dominions of the imagination know nothing of the metes and goals of that species of property which we call tangible and real in our popular and topsy-turvy conceptions of what is actually enduring.

To get more closely to my subject, in the days of the great queen, the English family-tree had not yet branched geographically into colonies and new teeming nations. It had not as yet split politically to fight out in parliamentary struggle and on the fields of civil war, those momentous questions of civil and political liberty in which Hampton and Cromwell but presaged Hamilton and Washington. While this cleavage began earlier, not to lose my figure, the gaunt and austere limb of Puritanism had not as yet struck forth into its portentous and uncompromising growth, and the family-tree of merry England was still gay with the blossoms of a happy careless life of wholesome enjoyment and fluttering the thousand leaves of young and vigorous living. Old England was the land of a youthful, hopeful spirit; a land of simple acquiescence in much: a paternal sovereign, accepted as one accepts one's father; a maternal church, loved, venerated, and for the most part unquestioningly obeyed, as good children hearken to a good mother. And there was what Shakespeare calls "degree" or recognized station in life, men who were lords and men who served them; men who tilled the soil while the barons determined matters politic by debate, or, more entertainingly, by battle. And there were men who served the church and those who adventured in commerce; while, as self-respecting and respected in their place, were artizans who made, chiefly by work of hand, the implements, the necessities, the luxuries which sustained and rendered beautiful this mechanism of a complex but accepted order of things. Contentment and pride in one's station in life is the dominant ground tone of this old civilization. In one of the old plays a yeoman, who had done conspicuous service for his king, bidden kneel to receive the honor of knighthood, beseeches his sovereign that he permit him to remain the man he is, and not raise him above his order!

> For 'tis more credit to men of base degree
> To do great deeds than men of dignity.

Perhaps there is something to say for pride to be to the full possibility of attainment the man you really are, rather than to seek, socially or otherwise, to appear — to be dubbed even — that which you really are not.

But acquiescence is only the ground note of our Elizabethan concerted harmony. And a second tone is that of an equally youthful spirit of adventure, the volatile element of which is the buoyancy of romance. Elizabethan adventure displayed itself in innumerable ways. This was the spirit that fitted out English ships to seek the northwest passage, that sent forth to shipwreck the brave and godly Sir Humphrey Gilbert, and Hendrick Hudson to abandonment in the gulf of his discovery. This was the spirit that opened frozen Muscovy to the western world; that threw down a gage to Spain and Portugal as to their claim of sovereignty over the tropics, that circumnavigated the globe. Of the essence of adventure were Drake's and other like "wars," forays and piracies in the Spanish main: her majesty of England hanging the unfortunate marauder who returned home empty-handed, and sharing royally in the spoils when success crowned these laudable efforts "to singe the beard" of his catholic majesty, Philip of Spain. And English prowess, plus a little help at first of the Dutch and much help thereafter of foul weather, defeated the powerful Armada, chased its fleeing and disheartened remnants to the Orkneys and around Ireland, achieving one of the greatest single adventures by sea of that or any age.

We, who learn of the old time mainly through books, forget how close were the men who wrote to action and the personal achievement of adventure. Spenser was one of the English oppressors of ever-oppressed Ireland, and he reaped the whirlwind in the destruction of his castle and the loss of a child in its flames; and Sir Walter Raleigh became a great historian only because, as a political prisoner in the Tower, he could not personally live the epics that he dreamed. When he was freed with a string for a few months by King James, it was to head an expedition to an imaginary El Dorado somewhere up the Oronoco River, and he returned to the block when his El Dorado, and his sovereign in consequence, failed him. Visionary and preposterous we may call such deeds, but they are veritably of the epic stuff, and the fine, careless, great-hearted spirit of romance ruled in them. Nor was Elizabethan adventure, all of it, visionary. Think of old Richard Hakluyt collecting, year after year, every account that he could find of foreign voyage, discovery and enterprise, by Englishmen or others, perfecting maps, lecturing on navigation, interviewing merchants and mariners, as eager to learn as to disseminate knowledge, and laying the foundations of the maritime empire of England, less with the ideal of bulging coffers than with that of an imperial leadership of mankind for the good of all. Startlingly prophetic is a passage of the courtly poet Samuel Daniel on the prospect of the English language,[1] where he says:

> And who, in time, knows! whither we may vent
> The treasures of our tongue, to what strange shores
> This gain of our best glory shall be sent,
> T' enrich unknowing nations with our stores?
> What worlds in th' yet unformèd occident
> May 'come refin'd with accents that are ours?
> Or who can tell for what great work in hand
> The greatness of our style is now ordained?

Farsighted, too, as to the possibilities, and as veritably an adventure, was Bacon's daring inventory of the universal stores of human knowledge and his prophetic device of a scientific method, the kernel of that precious thing which we call the ideal of research, a glimpse and a vision into a great and new era to come; and not less marvellous, in its totally different process, is the artistic mirroring of a world transfigured by the imagination in hundreds of personages, represented on the stage, which was Shakespeare's contribution, and that of his great fellow dramatists in lesser degree, to the imaginative adventure of his age.

Thus far I have endeavored to make clear that, among many other overtones — as the musician might express it — in the complex vibrations of Elizabethan life, the major notes were a simple, honest-hearted acquiescence, and a fine, careless, but often farsighted, romanticism, best expressed in the phrase, the spirit of adventure. These things, to my belief, are still the rul-

[1] From the poem *Musophilus*, aptly quoted by Courthope in his *History of English Poetry*, iii, 23.

ing qualities of that branch of the old Elizabethan race which, affiliating a hundred other strands to its own strong fiber, still vitally lives, flourishes and dominates in this our post-war, Anglo-Saxon America. And the first of our acquiescences is our maintenance of a democratic form of government, when personal representation, a necessity in true democracy, has long since become a matter impracticable by reason of the size of our empire and even of our individual states. Nothing better displays our inherited tractability and willingness to accept things as they are than our habitual forbearance in what is very often — I will not say always — the rule of the second best, recognizing, as we do, that in such a rule a safe average is most likely to be maintained and that, when all is said, we are not so very badly governed in the long run. Democracy is much like a clock. When in orderly condition the hands move forward telling, approximately at least, the hour of the day : though we do not even agree all the year as to that. They may speed up a little, though political clocks do not often do that; or lag behind a bit, as they are apt to do; but even when the clock of democracy stands still for twenty-four hours, have you noticed that the hands contrive to point right twice a day? There is much tampering with these fifty American time-pieces of ours and it is no wonder that they do not wholly agree; but the gods are always kind to one hundred millions of people, and perhaps among our other inheritances from our mother of England is that admirable faculty, so often proved in British history, the faculty of somehow muddling through.

In lucid intervals of reform, or even unreformed, I think that I can affirm that the American people, politically speaking, is a constitutionally contented people.

Secondly I feel that I can affirm likewise that ours is a religious people; though not a theological one. I rather admire the simplicity of heart that has actuated the legislature of Tennessee, followed by some other intellectually outlying states, as to the theory of evolution; although it reminds one somewhat of the celebrated case of Galileo. In the Elizabethan age belief was universal; and so was intolerance. Some of us still hate to see people saved by any other method but our own. The Elizabethans so devoutly believed in going to church — which always meant going to my church — that the law provided a heavy fine for non-attendance; on persistent neglect, transportation over seas; and capital punishment for the hardy offender who dared to return. Religiosity came into England with the Puritans, though they did not take all of it away with them when they went to Holland on their way to Boston. But I do not want to be flippant. It is the best of our sterling American virtues that we believe in God and worship at his shrines, that the homely virtues flourish unostentatiously among us, and that we have come to a respect for those who believe in a form of worship other than our own. Yes, the American is a religious people.

In the main, too, we seem to me a law-abiding people; perhaps about as much so as the subjects of Queen Elizabeth; certainly not more. The old age dealt drastically with the law-breakers. If their rank warranted the clemency, they were publicly and honorably beheaded on Tower Hill. If they were humble folk, they were only hanged at Tyburn, drawn, quartered and gibbeted in public places, as the French put it, "to discourage the others." We are not as law-abiding as the English have long since become. Assuredly good Queen Bess would have been amazed at the habitual difficulties of our courts in proving a scoundrel a scoundrel, and shocked at the readiness and frequency with which men and women separate under our " laws " — or rather opportunities of divorce. Elizabeth disliked married men and especially married clergymen. One of her bishops, the father of John Fletcher, she utterly disgraced, because he had the temerity to marry for a second time. And short would have been her royal shrift of a late American grand jury which could find no indictment because it did not happen to like the tenor of the law involved. No, we are not conspicuously law-abiding. Is it that we have to abide by too many laws? Perhaps if our minds were allowed some rest from the daily newspaper commentary on our depressing and singularly monotonous annals of crime, so that we could think of our people in the law-abiding rule, and not in the lawbreaking exceptions, we might cite our general observance of the law as still among our inherited virtues though still leaving much to be desired.

Let us turn now to the dynamo in our American life, its hope, its spirit of adventure, the romantic, the vital in us. For acquiescence is at best only a brake; and the substitution of a brake for a dynamo leads to many a stand-still in politics and in social and intellectual life. In several things the American temperament is much that of the Elizabethan. In it rules the spirit of youth, with its love of novelty, its detestation of slowness, and its impatience of restraint. We want results, not talk about processes. We prefer to trust intuitions rather than to be convinced by arguments; and we would rather be doing something wrong than be doing nothing at all. The war has taught us, much against our will, that professional and expert knowledge is really worthy of serious consideration; that, while you can take any farmer, or country lawyer, or small-town banker, and make a statesman out of him simply by sending him to Washington, you cannot do quite this same easy thing where winning battles is concerned or even altogether successfully when the winning concerns diplomacy. The Elizabethan age was precisely like ours in its childish confidence that any Englishman — or any American — can turn his hand to anything, in its ready, cheerful, heedless change of vocations — except as to mariners. Technical knowledge does seem somehow needful to the running of a ship: but not for the running of the ship of state. Faith that the ship of state will sail automatically and unerringly is a happy faith alike Elizabethan and American. The queen's celebrated favorite, the Earl of Essex, had no military training; and showed that he had had none in Ireland, as other gentleman declared a similar want again and again in the Low Countries and elsewhere. England is not the only country for which battles have been won by the grace of God and the valor of the common man.

The old age abounded in a fine, high-handed unscrupulousness born of the buccaneering habit. What the Elizabethan wanted, he took, whether from the Spanish King or anybody else; and generally he took it efficiently and sustained by a lofty sense of his inherent right to it because he wanted it so sincerely. This inherited trait is not lacking, today, in our elder brother of Great Britain; nor have we in America wholly outgrown it. Our late, great President Roosevelt knew that we needed the Panama Canal zone for the excellent — if somewhat Teutonic — reason that we could make a better use of it than its idle, stubborn possessors; and, in the best Elizabethan manner, we took it. Elizabethan piracy we have brought ashore and transferred into business, oil and land speculation; and our buccaneers occasionally attempt the pillage of the state as they did, somewhat less boldly, in the good old times. How natural it sounds to learn that the famous Sir Thomas Gresham, founder of the London Royal Exchange, grew rich in her majesty's services on his expenses and twenty shillings a day.[2] To the Elizabethan, as to our vital, active, capable men of affairs, business, politics, office and the quest of honors presented themselves in the guise of a great game of chance. Such people, while not altogether moral, are not niggardly nor meanly avaricious; it is the game, the chances, the excitement that attracts, the imaginative, adventurous, romantic spirit. Most of

[2] H. Hall, *Society in the Elizabethan Age*, 1888, p. 63.

the old adventurers were honest after their lights, but they could not let pass the chance to spoil the Philistine; and in most active affairs, with wit pitted against wit, cleverness, adroitness, address meeting its match, much of our advancement in the world comes in splendid moments of aphasia as to the golden rule. In the theogeny of the Elizabethans, the goddess Fortune sat higher than all the other gods, and faith in England's star of destiny was more powerful than belief in the thirty-nine or any other number of articles. The old age represented this glorious goddess of Fortune as a beautiful and imperious woman, presiding over a wheel by whose turn we mount to worldly felicity or are ground indiscriminately into the dust. Dame Fortune's American great-grand-daughter is a blonde "flapper," bobbed as to her head, carmined as to her lips, incessantly chewing gum; her name is Success and her emblem, the stock-ticker. It was their worship of success that made the Elizabethans imperialists; and it was they who were the first to recognize the sacred duty — and likewise the glorious possibilities — of "the white man's burden." It was this that made the Elizabethans jingoistic, causing them to make the lion roar on appropriate — and sometimes on inappropriate — occasions, much as we gloriously — and at times inopportunely — spread the beating wings of the American eagle and make him scream in tones more appropriate to a cormorant. Seriously, this splendid youthful spirit with its bustle, its noise, its certainties as to all things mundane and its faith in England, now in America, as the chosen of the earth, the best of mankind, is a magnificent and awe-inspiring phenomenon to contemplate. For it is based upon a reality, with all its vagaries and gaucheries, — the reality of worth, honest industry, faith in great ends and limitless aspirations. These are some of the things characteristic of the parent and the most vigorous of her offspring and it is these and other qualities as striking — which I cannot stop here to enumerate — that cause us to abound in a genuine patriotism, to dare, to succeed, to flourish in our capabilities and our achievements beyond our more cautious and more strictly rational neighbors.

One point in my comparison, there is left no time to discuss. Where, in all this cleverness and accomplishment of our American twentieth century, is that habit of seeing straight, that instinct for the essential truth, that inherent taste and devotion to beauty that begot the vision of *The Faery Queen,* the glory of Shakespearean drama and the limpid diction and sustained inspiration of our King James' translation of the Bible? I am not insensible of the essential soundness and greatness of newer literature in the English tongue. The Victorians — Tennyson, Browning, Dickens, Thackeray, Matthew Arnold and Carlyle — stand a mountain range of achievement, however we dwellers on the lowlands to which we have descended amid the towns of Galsworthy, Bennett and Shaw and even the heights of Barry or the garden of Yeats, seek to belittle what is behind us. And we had some American eminences of our own, though it is quite out of the fashion to remember Whitman, Longfellow, Emerson,

Hawthorne, or Poe. Without seeking an answer where complete answer, perhaps, there is none, I can not but feel that here, even, judged in the large, our individual tastes, even our demands as to the pleasure which literature and the arts can give may not fall so hopelessly below the elder age. Our life is not only infinitely more complex and infinitely more crowded, but our minds, whether as writers or as readers, are dissipated by a thousand momentary impressions — the newspapers, the advertisements, the transmission of trivialities over phone, telegraph, radio, and what not — so that the modern mind becomes jaded by mere contact and abrasion and is wearied without so much as a voluntary effort on our part. For the creation of great literature, at least, as for the lighting of a burning spark from the rays of the universal sun, there must be relentless concentration. The sun is still ours but the rays of his light are diffused over the countless objects that go to make up this heedless, headless modern life of ours. How can we who have scarcely time to think, plan, meditate, incubate and produce intellectually anything more than the foam and the froth that we churn up on the surface in the haste of our own rapid movement onward? — whither there is no time to inquire.

For those of us who have passed middle years, there is not much to say. What we have done — and left undone — is matter of the past, and we can neither learn nor, alas, forget. But there are those who are to follow us. I have been privileged now, for forty years, to know the American college boy, and many have been the satisfactory and happy hours that I have passed in his company, in the classroom and out. I have found him essentially honest, straight-forward, clean, intelligent and open to impressions. He responds unerringly to fair treatment, and expects it, as a matter of right. And he resents the effort to fool him, trick him, hating to be bossed or treated as an inferior. Possessed of his confidence, you can lead him anywhere — into the jaws of death, as the war disclosed to his immortal glory. But he will not be driven or coerced; and he dislikes — as who does not? — mere discipline with nothing to show for it. Our college boy is practical, adaptable, and he thinks for himself. He would not be his father's son if he did not look for material advancement and quick returns and more or less accept Dad's confusion of education with money, as something to be accumulated, like the parts of a machine, which, screwed up and wrenched together by somebody who gives his attention to screwing and wrenching, must be sure to run — or why should we pay out our money for it? But our college boy has another side too, the spirit of aspiration, the wish to know, the yearning after he cannot tell exactly what, with a desire to play his part honestly and fairly in the world and take without murmur the consequences of his own acts. This college boy of ours is representative of the youth of the nation, and with such material, looking at it in the large, the outlook is happy and nothing is impossible.

I do not personally know the American college girl so well, though I have had at least some of her age among her elder teaching sisters in my classes time and again. Our American college girl has come to stay; and I hope she will stay. She is able, tractable and earnest in her work, and gets full value out of what she undertakes. She does not play so hard as her brother and is more ready to accept what is told her; and occasionally will overwork — a thing that no healthy boy ever does. I am not unaware that much criticism has been recently current as to " our awful young people " and the incorrigibility of their ways. Measurably cloistered as I am, I do not much observe these dreadful things, and I have long since learned not to believe quite all that I hear. In one respect the easy social *camaraderie* among our boys and girls, as contrasted with the age of the chaperon, is a return to Elizabethan conditions which exemplify — as for example do the comedies of Shakespeare — an ease and naturalness in conduct among young people far wholesomer and sounder morally than that of the generations of gallantry and sentimentalism. I am personally an admirer of the Elizabethan type of heroine who, like Rosalind in *As You Like It,* or Beatrice who did for Benedick, is quite able to take care of herself and, at need, of the affairs of others, her friends, mere men like lovers, fathers and the like, about her. And I am glad to welcome her reincarnation in our new generation. But whether we like it or not they are ours, these young people, God bless them, or rather, we are theirs.

I am a stubborn optimist as to this America of ours. We are as yet, with all our stature, young, cross, wanting in tact, and not wholly civilized; but the greatest of all adventures is ours: ours is a country of opportunity, where all men — as yet, who are not brown — are welcome, where an unbounded generosity rules in our hearts despite all the predatory instincts of business, and disordered ideals of a disinterested leadership of the world still haunt our minds despite our massacre of our prophets. Much as I wish that some genius could devise for human government a means by which we might unerringly discover the veritable leaders among us to replace somehow this haphazard submission of the state to conditions of bickering and delay under which no one could run a peanut-stand successfully for a month, I am yet a devout believer in the common man and his everyday wife and in the sense, the sobriety, the judgment, more, the hopes and the aspirations, that are his and equally hers. In the tide of English life that first started the current of ours, there was first overweighted Puritanism, with its preoccupations with the horrors of the world to come and its effort to make this world anticipate them. This sort of Puritanism has for the most part sunk to the bottom of its own excessive weight. Secondly there was the careless, godless, thriftless spirit of the Cavalier. This has floated off for the most part on the surface, like a volatile oil, turning things about it for a moment to the colors of the rainbow, if fouling the surface. What remains in our American life is a strong, moving tide, able to carry on its bosom proud argosies, to tend ever onward, purifying as it flows, whatever the tributary streams that trouble its course for the moment, and tinge the clearness of its waters. With our experiment in free government a success, the world turns over a new page. Why then, O why, do we still shrink, and tremble to assume the moral, the spiritual, the intellectual leadership which is ours?

NOTE

I. Expanded from a paper read at the meeting of the Modern Language Association, December 1912. Abstract, *Publications* of that Society, xxviii, 1913.

II. A Review, *The Gownsman,* 1920.

III. Reprinted from *University of Pennsylvania Public Lectures,* vii, 141, 1921.

IV. Expanded from a Review in *The New York Evening Post,* iii, 5, 1922.

V. Rewritten from *Publications of the Modern Language Association,* xiii, 221, 1898.

VI. Reprinted from *A Book of Homage to Shakespeare,* London, 1916; also reprinted in *Proceedings of the American Philosophical Society,* iv, 471, 1916.

VII. Address before the Tudor and Stuart Club of Johns Hopkins University, reprinted in *The Graduate Magazine* of the same, September, 1923.

VIII. Reordered from *The University of Pennsylvania Law Review,* lxx, 141, 1922.

IX. Reprinted from *A Book of Seventeenth Century Lyrics,* 1899. (With kind permission of Messrs. Ginn & Co.)

X. Revised from *Modern Philology,* i, 31, 1903.

XI. Address before the English Speaking Union of Washington, D. C., April 24, 1926.

XII. Address before the Pennsylvania Historical Society, March, 1924.

INDEX OF NAMES AND TITLES

INDEX

Constable, Henry, 144.
Corneille, 111.
Cowley, Abraham, 148, 151.
Crashaw, Richard, 141, 143;
  Steps to the Temple, 147;
  148–151, 154, 155.

Daniel, Samuel, 74, 76, 101,
  106, 111, 113, 116, 201.
D'Annunzio, G., 7.
Davies, of Hereford, John,
  113.
Day, John, *Friar Rush,* 163,
  164.
Dee, Dr. John, 158.
Dekker, Thomas, 104; *If This
  Be Not a Good Play,* 164,
  165; *Old Fortunatus,* 166;
  173; *The Witch of Edmon-
  ton,* 177.
Derby, William Stanley, Earl
  of, 20, 192.
Dickens, 208.
Donne, John, 37, 65–67, 72,
  74, 82, 105, 113, 114, 155.
Dostoiefsky, 7.
Drayton, Michael, *The Poly-
  olbion,* 63; 76, 82; *Nym-
  phidia,* 169.
Droeshout, Martin, 28, 32.
Drummond, William, 36, 37,
  74, 82, 84.
D'Urfée, Honoré, his *L'Astrée,*
  122.
Drake, Sir Francis, 199.
Dryden, John, 38, 69, 70, 72,
  76–78, 80 81, 151.

Elizabeth, Queen, 67, 69, 102,
  105, 110, 112, 118, 121–123,
  142, 166, 181, 194, 203, 204.
Emerson, 208.
Essex, Robert Devereux, second Earl of, 205.

Fairfax, Edward, 84.
Fitzgeoffrey, Charles, 113.
Fletcher, Giles, 63.
Fletcher, John, 54–56; *The
  Tamer Tamed,* 103; 104,
  111, 204.
Fletcher, Phineas, 63.
Ford, John, 104, 173, 177.
Fraunce, Abraham, 113.
Frost, R., 197.
Furness, H. H., 52.

Galileo, 203.
Galsworthy, J., 208.
Garnier, Robert, 111.
Gascoigne, George, 61; *Sup-
  poses,* 86.
Gilbert, Sir Humphrey, 199.
Goethe, *Faust,* 160, 164.
Gorboduc, 110.
Gosson, Stephen, *The School
  of Abuse,* 62.
Greene, Robert, 50, 51, 54,
  160; *Friar Bacon and Friar
  Bungay,* 160, 161; *James
  IV,* 168; 170.
Greenwood, Sir George, 126,
  128, 129, 132, 135.
Gresham, Sir Thomas, 206.
Greville, Sir Fulke, 111, 112.
Grey, Lady Jane, 102.
Grim the Collier of Croydon,
  165.

216

INDEX

INDEX

Longfellow, H. W., 197, 208.
Lowell, J. R., 196.
Lust's Dominion, 169.
Lyly, John, *Euphues*, 8, 51; 110, 169, *Mother Bombie*, 173; 186, 192.

Macaulay, 181.
Machiavelli, 8, 164, 165; *The Marriage of Belphegor*, 166.
Maid's Metamorphosis, The, 169.
Malone, Edward, 127.
Marlowe, Christopher, 50, 51, 53, 54, 77, 110, 111; *Doctor Faustus*, 159, 160, 166; *Tamburlaine*, 159; 192.
Marston, John, 37.
Martial, 82.
Marvell, Andrew, 151, 152, 154, 155.
Massinger, Philip, 54, 106.
Mencken, H. L., *The American Language*, 195, 196.
Meres, Francis, 106.
Merry Devil of Edmonton, The, 162, 165.
Michelangelo, 12.
Middleton, Thomas, 55, 173; *The Witch*, 175; 176.
Milton, John, 63, 68, 69, 82; *Comus*, 114; 138, 139, 151, 155; *Samson Agonistes*, 156; *Paradise Lost*, 157; 197.
Moffatt, Dr. Thomas, 113.
Montemayor, 108.
Montgomery, Philip, Earl of, 27, 100, 115.

Montgomery, Susan, Countess of, 121.
More, The Play of Sir Thomas, 58.
Mornay, Plessis de, 117.
Munday, Anthony, *John a Kent*, 161; 162.

Nash, Thomas, 106.
Neilson, W. A., 28.
Newcastle, Margaret, Duchess of, 123.
Newcastle, William Cavendish, Duke of, 123.
Newman, J. H., 147.
Nider, J., *Formicarius*, 175.
Norris of Bemerton, John, 156.

Oxford, Edward DeVere, Earl of, 107, 192.

Parnell, Thomas, 151.
Pattison, M., 139.
Peele, George, 50, 51, 54.
Pembroke, Henry Herbert, Second Earl of, 100, 105, 106, 119.
Pembroke, Mary Herbert, Countess of, 100, 101, 105–107, 109–113; *Antonie*, 110; *Astrea*, 112; 115–119; *Discourse of Life and Death*, 117; *Psalms*, 117, 118; 122, 124.
Pembroke, William, third Earl of, 27, 100, 114, 115, 117.
Phelps, W. L., 182.

INDEX

INDEX

220

INDEX